Earth is a School

Earth is a School

William Wildblood

AXIS MUNDI
BOOKS

Winchester, UK
Washington, USA

JOHN HUNT PUBLISHING

First published by Axis Mundi Books, 2021
Axis Mundi Books is an imprint of John Hunt Publishing Ltd., 3 East Street, Alresford,
Hampshire SO24 9EE, UK
office@jhpbooks.com
www.johnhuntpublishing.com
www.johnhuntpublishing.com/axismundi-books

For distributor details and how to order please visit the 'Ordering' section on our website.

ISBN: 978 1 78904 791 2
978 1 78904 792 9 (ebook)
Library of Congress Control Number: 2020947470

A CIP catalogue record for this book is available from the British Library.

Design: Stuart Davies

UK: Printed and bound by CPI Group (UK) Ltd, Croydon, CR0 4YY
Printed in North America by CPI GPS partners

We operate a distinctive and ethical publishing philosophy in
all areas of our business, from our global network of authors to
production and worldwide distribution.

Contents

Also by William Wildblood

Meeting the Masters
978-1-78099-168-9 (Paperback)
978-1-78099-169-6 (ebook)

Remember the Creator
978 1 78535 927-9 (Paperback) 978 1 78535 928-6 (ebook)

This book is dedicated to my teachers in deep gratitude and the hope that it's some small return for their efforts. It's also dedicated to Michael Lord (1919-1999) their faithful servant, without whom I would have never encountered them nor been able to make the attempt to follow their teachings in the world.

Introduction

The title of this book comes from something I was told by my teachers more than forty years ago but it is the common understanding of anyone who understands that the purpose of life is spiritual – which is just another way of saying that life has a purpose. My encounters with these teachers is described in the book *Meeting the Masters* in which I relate how, between 1979 and 1999, I was spoken to by a group of spiritual beings who told me, when I asked them who they were, to think of them as messengers from God. Going by their manner and what they said, that seems an accurate description. Given that this was a critical part of my spiritual education I have included the text of a talk I recently gave on the subject as an appendix here.

However, this experience is incidental to the current book even if it could be seen as the root of it. In these pages I seek to address the age-old question "Why are we here?" The various religions offer their own answers to this but none, as they stand, seems entirely satisfactory. Modern science does not really look at the question, assuming there is no reason for us being here. We just are. But everyone must ponder the question at some time, as well as the associated questions "Where did we come from?" and "Where are we going?" You may have given up on the possibility of finding an answer and if you are hoping for any kind of definitive proof here you will be disappointed. Proof of spiritual matters is not part of the current curriculum. We have to work things out for ourselves on a spiritual level, not primarily (though it is included) an intellectual one. That means an element of faith is always going to be involved. It's a kind of entry test, an examination for the correct orientation of the heart, the heart meaning, in this instance, what we really are. But there are answers which can satisfy both logic and intuition and these are what we are going to examine in the current work.

The World is Perfect

One of the reasons people reject the idea of God is because of the many imperfections of the world. It is clearly not a place that is an ideal environment for its inhabitants as they seem to be, physical beings with emotional needs, and that is just the human inhabitants. Nothing in the world lives in a state of unalloyed peace and happiness, without challenge or difficulty. So, you might think this a strange claim to make but I think a case can be established for its truth, though we have to look at things in a slightly different way to usual.

At first glance, our material world is very far from perfect. There is suffering, there is pain, there is death. And yet a closer look can start to make sense of these negative aspects of our experience. I say a closer look, but it might be more accurate to talk of standing back and looking at the world as if from above, a great distance above.

If the world exists just for itself, then it is not perfect at all. Most of us would probably agree that there is more good than bad in it but there is still a lot of bad. This is a world of suffering. No wonder babies cry when they are born. However, what if the world does not exist for its own ends but is part of a much larger purpose? I submit that the aspect of reality we perceive as the physical world is but a small part of the whole and one that is the most restricted and limited. In these dimensions, material conditions enclose us and curtail our freedom. They are a permanent weight on our well-being, restricting us not only physically but also mentally. If reports of certain spiritual experiences are to be believed, the mind can work far better when it doesn't have to do so through the brain. It is more alert, more aware, wider open and better able to communicate its perceptions.

But here we are. We are in the world and it makes sense to

assume that here is where we are meant to be. For the moment anyway. We have a task to accomplish that we could not accomplish in one of the freer planes of existence. It is precisely the restrictions that work to our benefit here because they force us in certain directions. By making things harder for us, they require us to push. By pushing, we stretch ourselves and grow.

Therefore, this world can be seen as perfect for what it is intended to be or what we are intended to achieve in it. It is not a holiday resort but a training ground. You might almost think of it as a kind of assault course. It certainly has that aspect to it. If everything were easy for us and we never encountered difficulty or hardship or suffering, we might become like those spoilt children of rich parents who take everything for granted and assume that what they want they can always have. They don't grow unless they are made of very good stuff to begin with, and even then their growth might be limited for without struggle you really don't have much incentive to change or grow.

So, when I say that the world is perfect, I am not saying that is good or could not be better. But I do say that for its purpose, it is right. It provides the right environment for spiritual growth because we have to confront difficulty. Here we are faced with good and evil and have to choose. We are not given direct evidence of God but have to find that ourselves and, in finding, we make it our own. It becomes part of our inner being, not just something we see out there like the sun. We all believe in the sun but that doesn't make us radiate light or warmth. But when you build the belief of God into yourself by your own volition, then you start to become like God. It's a long process but you really do start to do just that.

And so, this world with all its many imperfections is perfect as a school for evolving consciousness. Indeed, it is the imperfections that make it perfect. Suffering teaches us to overcome suffering in ourselves and respond to it in others.

The possibility of sin helps us to identify tendencies to sin within ourselves and therefore be able to root them out.

The reader may question my use of the word perfect to describe the world as that suggests something complete and unimprovable in itself, and it is true that I am just using this word to make a point; that being why is this world not perfect if God is a loving God? But if the imperfections of this world are more conducive to spiritual growth than a seemingly perfect environment would be and if spiritual growth is the actual reason for this material world in the first place then we can surely regard the world as ideal for what it is meant to achieve? The world is traditionally regarded as fallen so it is nowhere near what it could or should be, and yet the truth is that if we were better, then it would be too. To a large extent, the imperfections of the world reflect our own imperfections, hard as that might be for the materialistic mind to conceive, and they come about in order to teach us to overcome these imperfections. Pain and suffering have their part to play in the growth of consciousness. We can respond to them with anger and resentment or humility and acceptance and if we choose the latter path, they can have the effect of deepening our thoughts and opening our hearts. This is where free will comes in. It enables us to use the difficulties of the world as a springboard to spiritual growth.

To be creative and capable of development the perfect must have the imperfect within it. It is in this sense that our world is perfect.

* * *

If we would understand the reason for life in this world, we must see it as a place for growing souls. It is designed for the development and testing of human beings so that they may become fully-fledged sons and daughters of God, able to function in the fullness of love and creativity. This doesn't mean the world and the things in it are not real, but they are not permanent, not as they appear to be here, anyway. The idea that this world is not its own justification has led some to think of it as illusion, but the only illusion is to take it on its own terms. The world is real enough, but it is not as it seems.

The fact that the world is an environment for spiritual growth explains much about it that puzzles us, both materialists who cannot see any sign of a divine maker, and spiritually oriented people who wonder why a divine maker would allow evil, suffering, injustice and so on. But these test and challenge us. They potentially bring out incipient qualities which would otherwise remain dormant. A perfect world such as we may assume heaven to be would be a world in which the sort of growth we need, as we are now, would not be possible. To grow a muscle, you need to encounter physical resistance. To grow a soul you need to encounter spiritual resistance, which is adversity.

That does not mean evil is God's will. Temporary separation from God is God's will but this separation will eventually bring about a conscious return if we react to it in the way we should. Evil is a spiritual aberration which can be used by God to further his purposes, but God is not directly responsible for it. It's the result of wrong choices made by beings to whom the freedom to make wrong choices so that they could consciously make right ones, as opposed to not having any other alternative, has been given.

God hides from us in this world so that we have to find him. He sometimes hides in plain sight, but he is not an obvious fact of consciousness which cannot be denied. "Seek and ye shall find, knock and the door shall be opened" is in one sense an obvious instruction but in another it is deep wisdom. You may not find straightaway but if you persevere, thus proving the sincerity of your search, you will surely find at least enough to help you continue your search.

There is no lasting happiness in this world because there is not meant to be. If we were content with what we have, we would cease to grow and waste our lifetime. But there is also no lasting happiness here because the only thing that can provide true lasting happiness is God himself. Nothing else endures because everything else is temporal. Only God is eternal.

The materialist denies God because he cannot see him but he cannot see him because he is not looking with the proper organ of perception. That would be faith and imagination which, in the higher aspects of these two apparently separate things, is one thing. Where faith and imagination join there is truth. Faith without imagination is dry and sterile, spiritually speaking. Imagination without faith may be creative after a fashion but it is destructively so. Its products do not enhance and enrich life. They do not add to it and end up corrupting it. The world is the most marvellous creation because it fulfils its function of a spiritual training ground to perfection. Yes, this world is perfect. Not perfect as in supremely good but perfect as in ideal for its purpose. The imperfection of this world points to the perfection of God.

The Soul

To describe the physical world as a training ground inevitably means we have to reassess what a human being actually is. No longer can we regard it as what it appears to be and is popularly supposed to be. It must come from elsewhere and have its origin in a higher sphere of being. If earth is a school, it has a purpose beyond itself and we humans are called to a life that is more than the one we currently experience. But we are not yet fit for that life. We have to be trained for it. This is the spiritual worldview.

One of the most interesting things my teachers told me was that **"the greater part of you remains with us"**. What can this mean? They lived in spiritual realms which they described as **"places of poetry, music and colour where the vibrations were much higher than on the earth plane"**. This is the world of the soul, which is the spiritual component of our being, created by God. It is here that we are, so to speak, based and from where we descend to the earth plane. The soul is an individual unit of consciousness, formed by God out of his own self but endowed with free will so that it may eventually become godlike itself. For this to happen it must evolve, which means develop its innate spiritual nature, grow the seed that is within it. This it cannot do on its own level, which is a world without challenge or the means to confront difficulty. It must descend to earth. The idea of descent is symbolically accurate as it represents a stepping down of consciousness into restriction and a condition in which the objective world is experienced as totally separate from inner consciousness. Substance thickens to bring about the experience of duality, a splinter in previously known un-self-aware oneness, but this gives inchoate mind the environment it needs to awaken and begin to come to terms with itself as an organ of self-conscious thought.

7

The soul is created as a baby, something undeveloped but with potential to grow. It must then create itself as a proper self, with agency. You might say that God makes an unfinished product. The material world is the environment designed for the purpose of bringing about the completion of the work. But the design of this world is rudimentary. Certain laws have been set up from the start and these are allowed to take their effect as the beings, both human and others, but principally human, which is to say self-conscious, introduced into the environment interact with it. The world is made as a habitat for us in which we can grow and express ourselves but, in so doing, we also add our contribution as sub-creators. This does not just refer to building material things. We also affect the world through our thoughts and emotional reactions. It is not that we create our own reality, but we certainly contribute to it. Creation is of God but can be altered by human behaviour. There is an objective reality but there is also an ongoing interaction of this with the human mind.

* * *

When my teachers told me that "**the greater part of you remains with us**" they were referring to the soul. Note that they call it the greater part. They do not call it the real part or the true part. The earthly personality, the, in my case, William Wildblood part, is part of what we are but it is not the whole of what we are. This is why, for some people, the world seen in its own light does not seem completely real and nor do they, as they appear to be, seem completely whole. This is definitely not implying it is all an illusion. That is not the case. But both the world and the incarnate person are but the outermost parts of something more substantial. The illusion is to identify this world with the whole world and yourself solely with your outer parts, meaning mind as well as body. For instance, I don't think the person called William Wildblood is my whole self. He is real enough, but he only represents a limited aspect of the true self. He is the expressed part on Earth of something more fundamental. A few people identify themselves largely with their bodies. Many more identify themselves with their minds, their thoughts, desires and so on. But the true self is a spiritual being of which the earthly self is but a projected part, something like a multi-dimensional thing squeezed into a three-dimensional pot. It is the phenomenal representative of a spiritual being.

Even many people who call themselves spiritual identify with their material selves and worldly personality. They seek to make that better. But this approach can lead to a kind of materialistic spirituality in which the earthly ego is regarded as the one to be saved, when in fact it is the earthly ego and its goals and desires that must be put in their place before anyone can be born again in the spirit.

The soul or higher self is our real spiritual being, the central sun, which sends down a ray of itself to the physical world in order to gain the experience of life in matter, which it needs in order to grow. As the old adage has it, it is separation that leads to completion. You need to break up unity in order to become aware of unity. This earthly representative of the soul in matter consists of mental, emotional and physical parts but with connections to higher levels, principally through the conscience and the imagination, that can be opened up and developed with proper practice and right motivation.

It is probable that the soul on its own level cannot grow or cannot grow in as comprehensive a way as it can in the physical world, where it is largely on its own so obliged to develop its mental side and also become a full individual therefore more independent and freer. So, we need to leave the spiritual security of the soul to become fully conscious of it and to develop its creative powers. This we do through the earthly personality, but that is more the vessel for our endeavours. It should not be the main focus for them. At the same time, to regard the earthly personality as spiritually irrelevant and as something to be left behind is also wrong. The idea is to combine the two. They are both part of our whole self. Nevertheless, it is the soul or higher self that is the centre of our true being. That is the core of our identity.

Freedom

If Earth is a school, what's it a school for? The answer to that is basically simple. It's a school for turning men into gods. In other words, it's a school for consciousness. Consciousness just means having the ability to be conscious and there are grounds for thinking that everything has this in some degree, however limited it may be. But only humans have self-consciousness and this Earth is a school for turning that into divine awareness, in which the created soul becomes a fully-fledged creator itself, able to express the triple qualities of Will, Love and Intelligence in complete form.

A god must be self-conscious. Anything not self-conscious has no freedom and freedom is the defining characteristic of divine being. It is the source of creativity and the necessary background to love. With that in mind, let us examine this extraordinary quality a little.

Nothing else that we know of in the world is free, but a human being is. That does not mean we are totally free. We are conditioned and determined by many things, hereditary things, environmental things, our biology, our experiences and so on. Nonetheless, at the core of our being there is a freedom that is recognised by all sensible people, known instinctively to be there at a level beyond the purely phenomenal one. This is the basis of our individuality. It is what makes us who we are. It potentially makes us free of nature or matter which are determined things and offers us a way into the true and unlimited creative freedom of the spirit.

Where does this freedom come from? It cannot come from matter because everything material is conditioned by what it is made of. It's a product of other things which define it. There is no freedom in matter. No one really knows what goes on at the sub-atomic level, but it is not freedom. Therefore our freedom

11

must be non-material or spiritual, which means it comes from God or else it is innate in spirit itself. But spirit is freedom before it is even being which is another way of saying that it is "I" not "it", personal not impersonal.

The personal nature of God or spirit (I don't really differentiate except that you could say the one is transcendent and the other immanent) has important implications for what this world is for. It is a place in which we may exercise our freedom. That is why it is a place in which suffering and evil exist. Our life is a series of choices leading up to the all-important choice of God or not God. If we choose God, we choose the creative freedom of spirit, light, love and truth. If we choose not God, we choose matter. Effectively, we choose prison and darkness but so that the choice may really be free these can be seen by the mind rebelling against God as freedom and light. However, it is freedom for the ego which is the product of the spiritual self identifying with matter. This unrepentant ego then goes to what we can call hell, but hell is only seen as hell by the soul that has chosen God and spiritual freedom. To the soul that goes there it may well be just a place of experience, albeit limited experience, like any other. The eternal privation would only be felt as such, to the fullest degree anyway, by the soul that has given itself back to God in love. For the soul that has denied God, the loss of God is not so keenly felt even though it will certainly be known on some level.

It may be that, spiritually speaking, freedom is more fundamental even than love because love is only possible as a result of freedom. It is also the case that the freer you are, the more you love but this refers to true spiritual freedom not mere self-will. The devil has self-will, but he lost his real freedom when he rejected God. Complete freedom is only possible in God because God is the Father of freedom. It is what he is.

I said that suffering and evil come about because of freedom, which raises the question as to how we may overcome the one but keep the other. The way is through Christ. That wonderful statement in the Book of Common Prayer that 'in his service is perfect freedom' sums up the truth that material bondage can only be broken when we freely align ourselves with the spiritual reality of Christ. At the moment, we have freedom, but we are still largely bound. In Christ that limited freedom becomes full and complete. At the beginning, we were one with God but not consciously so. Through being born in a place in which the ability to exercise freedom is possible, a place of duality, where inside and outside are fully separate, we can consciously choose God but this choice is not just an intellectual thing. It must be a redirection of our whole being from material to spiritual. This is why the path back to God is a hard one. It requires complete reorientation of the will.

Freedom is why God made both us and the world. It is what lies behind creativity and gives the universe its dynamic quality. Correctly used, it is our passport to becoming a god but at the moment many of us are giving it up by surrendering to evil, the very reverse of what should be. We must break the chains of material bondage and claim our freedom in the world of spirit.

Humanism

This book has its basic theme, but it will take little detours now and again as and when that seems appropriate. A school has different subjects and the spiritual life has various different aspects to it, not all of which are always given enough attention even by those who feel they have a calling to that life.

We live in unprecedented times. In one sense, extending the school analogy, it could be that we are taking end of term examinations, maybe even end of school examinations. The spiritual life is always full of tests but today there is a major test for the whole of humanity. Summed up, it is this: God or self. We must all choose.

In many traditions there is the concept of the end times, when spirit is denied, truth inverted, and materialism dominates. That time surely is now. We have abandoned a spiritual outlook, unless that can be trimmed down and fitted into a fundamentally secular worldview, and we have put self ahead of God. This is what I mean by surrendering to evil. That might be considered an excessive way of describing the matter, but evil is a spiritual (not divine) reality and, as Jesus said, if you are not actively for him, you are against him. In the spiritual world there is no neutral ground. There is good and there is that which is not good and that is evil.

Modern man has chosen to deny God and substitute for that reality the invented philosophy of humanism. Humanism is, in one form or another, our modern religion but it is a religion without a God and without transcendence, so one that is incapable of saving or transforming, which is the proper function of religion. And that's not its only problem. Despite its avowed aim of ennobling man, humanism actually degrades him because it denies that in him which raises him beyond the natural world. Its rejection of God takes away our status

14

as a spiritual being come to Earth and at a stroke abolishes the sense of higher and lower (closer to God or further away from him), reducing the human soul to a mere by-product of material forces. Then, with its ostensibly noble goal of seeking to eradicate suffering, humanism isolates man in this world, banishing him from his true home in the spiritual realm. This is because the reality of tragedy in this life which so offends the utopian humanist comes from the fact that we are part animal and part angel. It is the conflict between these two aspects of our being that is responsible for suffering at a level beyond the purely physical. If you get rid of tragedy, you get rid of the spiritual. It is obviously not wrong to address the fact of suffering but to seek to remove the possibility of it altogether as seems to be the humanist end goal would be to kill the human soul.

This is not meant as an excuse to ignore suffering but an attempt to show the inner cause and even, up to a point, the spiritual necessity of it. Suffering is mysteriously tied up with love. If you remove the possibility of the one, you also remove the possibility of the other. It is likely that we only really love in the spiritual sense to the degree that we either have suffered or are able to suffer. I have often remarked on the fact that the faces of the people I regard as the most spiritually mature are those that have suffering etched into them. Suffering gives depth, not inevitably but it can do, depending on how one reacts to it. You can react with acceptance and faith and this brings you closer to God or you can become embittered and rail against heaven for its, as you perceive it, injustice, but this just drives you deeper into the ego. The fact of suffering is a spiritual problem for many people, but imagine a world without suffering. Would we have anything to drive us to a higher state? Might we just remain satisfied with the material world and thereby cut ourselves off from the deeper truths of the spirit? And what would there be to cleanse us of sin and bring us naked and humble before God as eventually we all must be? Many people abandon faith in God because of the fact of suffering and evil in this world but you could equally well say that they demonstrate God's existence because they point to a world beyond this one. Would we feel the offence of evil so much unless we understood at some level that reality was good?

When Man tries to become more than Man by himself, he becomes less than Man. Without the idea that he is a son of God, in his deepest nature a being not of this world, he can never go beyond himself. And yet the essence of true humanity is that we can go beyond our earthly selves. That reality lies behind all our greatest achievements and best ideas of ourselves and our place in the universe. However, if we are to go beyond ourselves, we cannot do that as ourselves as we experience ourselves to be now. We have to see ourselves as spiritual beings not earthly ones. The great mistake of many religious people is to think that they can take their earthly self, their normal human self, intact to heaven. Not so. All spiritual teachers who know what they are talking about have proclaimed that it is not change but transformation we need. In the humanist conception of man, transformation is impossible because the human being is a material being only. Matter cannot change into spirit unless spirit is already present as the underlying reality.

Humanism has led to the smashing of the hierarchy of good. We no longer recognise the higher as higher or the lower as lower because we no longer recognise God as God and what the reality of God actually means. Without God as the highest reality the ladder of being is levelled to the ground and qualitative differences are negated. Humanism, which ostensibly sought to raise man, has only succeeded in dragging him down. Looking at the present situation in the world, that process is still taking place. We are being dragged further down. If man does not know himself to be potentially a god, does he then become just another beast? It would seem from current events that may be precisely what happens.

Some humanists think we will evolve to a higher state of consciousness, but fail to understand that evolution in this sense only brings out what is already there. It doesn't come from nothing as the higher cannot come from the lower. Even more foolish, indeed inhuman, are the transhumanists who imagine that by melding man and machine they can create a higher being. If they ever succeed in this unholy operation, they will find they have only created a living hell.

Human beings have tried innumerable ways to reach heaven without acknowledging the reality of God and Christ because they have not been willing to make the sacrifice this entails. But it is a good sacrifice that only requires the giving up of our spiritual sickness. The unrepentant ego is like a cancer and it must be cut out. There is some pain in this, but the alternative is death. Humanism is the path that leads to death. Yes, man is a noble creature with unlimited potential but only when he takes his place as a son of God. Without God man is not much more than a vainglorious braggart swollen with self-importance but inwardly empty.

The Nature of Evil in the Modern World

One of the major tests of the present time is to do with the ability to discern between spiritual good and spiritual evil. The test is made harder by the fact that these are not what they appear to be if you go by general consensus. We are being examined at a deeper level than that of the surface mind. In this school, especially now, you can't always trust those who present themselves as the teachers.

It is often asked how the Germans in the 1930s could have been taken in by Nazi propaganda and gone along with its programme. One might ask a similar question today. How can so many people not see the anti-spiritual insanity of the present time? How is it that we do not just accept but often actively celebrate contemporary evil? The answer presumably is, we don't recognise it as evil. But why is that? It is because we don't know, or don't wish to know, the true purpose of life or what a human being actually is. We don't (or won't) think of ourselves as souls, but as material beings whose material needs, desires and goals are primary. Modern evil is the refusal to recognise truth. It is the rejection of God and his replacement with a worldly ideology that equates good with what leads to mortal happiness and evil with what causes suffering to mind or body. But as most people once knew, certainly most people who framed the pattern of civilisation, good is what leads to the development of the soul and brings Man closer to God and evil is what separates Man from God. By that criterion, we are among the most evil people to have existed anywhere ever.

Think about this for a moment. We imagine ourselves as enlightened, compassionate, caring human beings, but in point of fact we have egotistically (and it is the unrepentant ego that is behind this) rejected the reality of what we are. If all good is in God, and it is because God is Truth, and we have abandoned God, that makes us evil. There are no two ways about this, and I believe that we know it. We don't accept it, but we do know it at a level of our being that we keep suppressed. We know it because God is inside us, every one of us, and speaks to us of his presence if we allow it. If we don't hear his voice that is because we don't want to. I know that many people would say they do want to but can't and I'm afraid all I would say to that is, try harder. I realise it is difficult in this modern world when so much is against it. The whole culture is against it and all the religions are pale shadows of what they once were, but let me make two points to support my assertion.

First, it is more and more apparent that a world without God is heading for utter disaster. Everyone recognises this or should. If they don't, they are either too young and time should bring understanding or else they are too besotted by shallow worldly pleasures or caught up in political ideologies that pander, in one form or another, to the ego. I apologise if that seems extreme but it's time for straight-talking. People who are ready to understand will understand. Those who are not perhaps need to suffer a little before their minds are receptive to reality. Sad to say that is no one's responsibility except their own.

The second reason that we are not left spiritually bereft even in this age of triumphant materialism is that today, more than ever, there are teachings to suit a wide variety of tastes and intellectual proclivities readily available. There are many people writing, talking and so on about the evil of the present times. Most, admittedly, do not have a high public profile but anyone who sincerely wishes to find truth will be directed towards someone who can help them. This someone may just be a steppingstone to something else of greater truth but the point is guidance is there if you search for it.

Evil is subtle and always attacks in ways we least expect and the areas where we are weakest. So my teachers told me and so I have found. The Nazi form of evil is clearly a non-starter in the West nowadays despite sections of the press being concerned with far-right extremism. We are too familiar with it. But the evil that pervades the Western world now presents itself as good and this is the evil we have succumbed to and we have done so because of the evil within ourselves. That is how it always works. Our own shallowness and egotism is reflected in the world we have created which, in turn, feeds back into the shallowness and egotism.

It is the materialist who defines evil in material terms, violence, murder, rape and so on. All these things certainly are evil. That is not being denied. The material world is part of the totality of reality. But it is not the only part. Reality is primarily spiritual and the contemporary attack on the soul is every bit as evil as the evil of the Nazis. It is just evil manifesting in a different sphere, spiritual rather than material. Our refusal to recognise spiritual evil and the hubris that goes along with this is why the Western world is dying. It cannot be saved but that is not important. What is important is individual souls, and these can be saved but only if they renounce the world as it is and do what I believe is called, in the terminology of electronic devices, a factory reset in which all or most of the accumulated data is wiped clean and you start afresh. This is repentance or, to use a word I prefer because it signifies something more comprehensive and deep rooted, metanoia, a total change of mind and heart driven by penitence.

The need for metanoia means that a vague, generalised, intellectual kind of spirituality is not the answer. There's plenty of that about but it does not reach to the bottom of the soul and can often be engaged in without the renunciation of worldliness. It's a new suit of clothes when we need a new mind. The true religious goal is not to make us happy in this life but to prepare us to enter the next. The point of life is to know how to die. Too much contemporary spirituality is therapeutic when it should be transformational, and this is part of the form evil currently takes in our world.

* * *

Once we understand the nature of how evil manifests itself in the modern world, we have to ask how it got there. Is this just something human beings have come up with themselves as they have developed over the past few centuries and become (in line with divine intention one should say) more intellectually focused and with a greater sense of their own agency? Or is there some exterior power that has fostered this and to which we have succumbed? If so, does this power have its own agenda which would be to do with diverting human beings away from their proper spiritual destiny into a more materialistic, atheistic form of consciousness which separates them from God? Obviously, nothing can be fully separated from God as he is the life within all being, but it is possible for a self-aware creature to intensify the self-aware aspect of its nature to the point at which its divine source is effectively negated. As is often said, hell is separation from God.

Framing the question like this gives us the answer. Many people have observed that the spiritual corruption of humanity has moved forwards in gradual phases over such a long time span, but always in the same direction, that there must be some over-arching plan with a long-term goal, not possible in the human context, behind it. Call this a conspiracy theory if you like but know that the conspiracy is of a supernatural order and not human, though it will have its agents, usually unaware of their function, on the human plane.

There is no earthly conspiracy masterminded by some Illuminati group or, if there is, they don't have that much power and are not the real source of spiritual destruction. On the other hand, there is a spiritual conspiracy orchestrated from a place beyond the physical world and the beings involved use any such groups for their own purposes. These groups would be discarded and sacrificed once they have served those purposes. Thus, the global lockdowns of 2020 were not cooked up in some secret hideout by politicians, bankers, corporate businessmen and such like intent on a political takeover, but by demons working for the spiritual destruction of human beings. This is why governments could seemingly almost stumble into them, obviously with no real plan except self-preservation and the desire to be seen to be doing the right thing. It's why so many factors, virus, media frenzy, 'the science' (most modern scientists are just relatively high IQ technocrats not the truth seekers of the past), a culturally decadent population and so on all came together in the way they did to bring about a particular result.

This may sound sensationalist but it has been the common religious understanding for a very long time, and the fact of demonic attack on the human soul has only been lost sight of over the last couple of centuries as the devil faded from public view, the more effectively to carry out his designs. He has done this so well that most people now live lives in which God has no place. He is not just pushed out from the centre where he should be. He is barely acknowledged at all other than in a most perfunctory and more or less meaningless way. The essence of evil is not in doing obviously evil things but in denying God, and that is the principal evil of the present day. Naturally, from the denial of God many other things proceed, actions and thoughts, modes of behaviour, ideologies and beliefs that embed that denial deeper into consciousness and cause a greater separation between a person who holds to this way of life and that person's spiritual source.

Most people today do not actively pursue obviously evil ways. After all, and not meaning to be facetious, that does require quite a bit of effort. But two things indicate our tendency to spiritual evil. These are our alienation from God and growing self-centredness. To be sure, we are constantly enjoined to think of others but this is largely superficial if the point from which we are doing it is ego-bound and does not look beyond itself for the true reality of what it is. We can either look for our true being in God or we can find it in self. It is this latter which means that so many people of the present day have fallen into spiritual evil.

Transformation

The process of making gods out of men is illustrated in the New Testament in the context of Jesus's first miracle. It was at the wedding feast at Cana where he turned water into wine. Water represents basic everyday consciousness. It is simple and ordinary, but it is also absolutely fundamental to life. Everything Jesus did has symbolic value and it is not coincidence that he made wine from water as opposed to dust or some other substance. It was a miracle, but one that did not go against nature so much as speed up a natural process. Wine has water as its essential constituent, but something more than water has been formed. Water symbolises life in the physical world, but wine is spiritual life. The transformation was a natural spiritual operation.

It is also significant that this miracle took place at a wedding. Cosmically speaking, a wedding is the union of the two polar forces in the universe of spirit and matter which brings about new life. It is the perfect expression of love and creativity and, incidentally, reveals how foolish present debates about equality between the sexes are. On one level, the two sexes are equal because both are essential to the manifestation of being. On another level, they are different and must be to fulfil their respective tasks, so the idea of equality is meaningless. As usual nowadays, we have materialised a spiritual truth and thereby completely distorted it. This is what happens when theory and abstract thinking take over from common sense, instinct and intuition.

Turning water into wine is what the earthly school is all about. The basic raw material of human consciousness is planted in the earth, where the spiritual equivalents of sun and rain do their work. We might think of them as environmental pressures and experience. But, as you would expect, there is a critical difference between grape and human. In the latter case, external factors on their own will not perform the task. There needs to be active cooperation from the soul if it is to evolve, that is, unfold its potential. Each individual must make him or herself, and this involves developing the qualities of the innate individual character through self-expression, but also consciously opening up the mind to the spirit of God. God fills the soul only to the extent that the soul has emptied itself of itself. But only a developed self has the spiritual wherewithal, the capacity, to receive and understand and properly express the divine substance. Of apparent paradoxes such as this is the spiritual path formed.

The school is a school of transformation but for long periods nothing much seems to happen. Many people mistake sudden bursts of spiritual energy for permanent states, only to fall back into the same old state of mind when these have passed. Then they perhaps try to prolong the experience by becoming teachers. But the transformation does not and is not intended to take place in this world, despite stories of permanent enlightenment. This world is the school in which lessons take place and like any school it is about learning. The holidays come afterwards – provided one has taken the course and succeeded in the passing out exam.

Water into wine, base metal into gold, alchemical transformation. The material is consciousness and the work is development, purification, transcendence. In Biblical terms, we can describe this as the transforming of an Adam into a Christ. Christ is the template of perfection, which does not mean that we can all be him but we can all become like him by partaking in his divine life. He is the reality which we can emulate through a kind of spiritual osmosis. Esoterically considered, this is what eating the flesh and drinking the blood of the Son of Man really means. It means becoming like him through absorbing his life, but we can only do that to the extent that we have purified the inner vessel that is our own soul. The real flesh and blood of Christ is his divine nature, which we access through the creative imagination, and which, when consumed, alters the mind, even its very structure, eventually transforming it from a dense material state to one of spiritual illumination.

The evolution of consciousness is the process that turns Adam into Christ. That is to say, a new formed spiritual being into a fully functioning son of God. The journey is one from innocence to experience and then back to innocence again, but this time as a self-conscious state with all the fruits of experience, will, intellect, creativity and so on, added.

The early adamic state is when the newly created individual is not yet conscious of his individuality. He is one with nature and his environment. He is one with spirit as it is manifested in nature but totally ignorant of his Creator, the transcendent God. So, he has to leave the paradise of union with the Mother principle in order to know the Father. This means he has to experience the sense of separation and become conscious of duality, and that, of course, introduces the possibility of pain and suffering in a more than merely physical sense. So, he has to discover himself as a person and a true individual. Alone but also free. Early man lived in what we now call a participation consciousness. It was a state of unity, but natural not spiritual, meaning that the union was an unconscious one with what you might describe as the anima mundi, not a fully conscious union of love with the Creator. Thus, Adam fell in order to know himself. Whether this fall was intended or not is an interesting point. My belief is that it was not, not in the way that it happened, anyway. Adam was meant to evolve in a gentler fashion, one in which death and suffering would not have played so great a part. However, the process was disrupted in the way mythologically presented in the book of Genesis, and sin entered in. God had to remake his plans for the evolutionary path, but he has to do this constantly in response to the exercising of human free will, anyway. He may have a plan, but it is not fixed. It is an organic thing, always growing and changing according to how human beings react to it and what they instigate. There is destiny and there is free will and the two necessarily interact at every moment as life unfolds. Consequently, God's plan alters second by second, according to events, but its direction remains constant. Yet we need to remember that all this occurs only in time. There is also the timeless state in which everything that ever happens is known to the mind of God in an eternal present. However, it would be a mistake to conflate the two modes of being, temporal and atemporal.

Whether or not the Fall was part of God's original plan (or, most likely, anticipated but not intended), it has happened, and we are here as a result of it. We have fallen but we can rise again. The first step in that though is to recognise that we have fallen, and this modern man stubbornly refuses to do. There is no doubt that in our journey from spirit to matter and back to spirit again, we have reached the nadir. Like the prodigal son, we must turn around and head for home. All the fruits of a separated consciousness that we have gained we must now put in the service of a higher path, one of the journey back to the Creator. But, as a group, the human race shows no signs of doing this, which explains the truly dangerous situation in which we find ourselves at present. There are forces which will make every effort to keep us in darkness, either by convincing us that there is no God or else distorting our ideas about him in ways that might serve them. If our hearts were pure, we would see through this because a pure heart sees truth. But our hearts are not pure, and they will not be so without repentance, the honest acknowledgement by each individual that he is a sinner. There are two things required for this. The awakening to a love for the good, the beautiful and the true, and a genuine sense of unworthiness. This is not a self-flagellating attitude, which is generally a sign of egotism but a right and proper humility before our Creator.

We must turn the corner. We have experienced the fullness of the stage of conscious separation. There is nothing more to be gained from that, and everything to be lost if we continue down that path. But when we search for oneness, we must do so in the right way. Currently there are many people and groups who respond to oneness but who do so incorrectly. What they do is seek it on a horizontal level but it is not there and if it is sought there, all that will be found is a false or artificial oneness, an unnatural oneness, a reflection of the oneness of unqualified base matter. It must be vertically understood, that is to say, we must seek connection to God, and only then will we be able to relate to our fellow men and women in the right way. If we try to establish oneness without doing so in the light of God, all we create will be oppressive because the horizontal level is that of expression, hence one of difference, hierarchically ordered. Oneness can only be in God, and it is to that we must turn. The Masters told me that there are many teaching half-truths at present. Nowhere is this more obvious than in ideas about oneness which are distorted and misinterpreted by being applied where they should not be and ignored where they should be operative.

The journey of spiritual evolution is one that can be described as going from savage to sage on the one hand and sinner to saint on the other. It goes from a state of unself-conscious oneness to conscious separation to conscious oneness. On the face of it, this might appear to conflict with conventional religious teaching, whether of East or West, but I believe it finds a place within that since it simply looks at the same question, how to put unregenerate man right with God, from a different perspective and through a longer lens.

Cycles of Change

In his book *The Order of the Ages* (Sophia Perennis, 2001), which I recommend to anyone interested in the subject of this chapter, the author Robert Bolton gives the dates of the Kali Yuga as being from 3102 BC to 2082 AD. If you want to know how he arrives at those dates you must read the book but, suffice it to say here, his reasons for them seem plausible enough. For those not familiar with the term Kali Yuga, it refers to the last of four ages in Hinduism during which the world gradually descends from a natural spiritual state into materialism and disconnection from the divine order. This particular form of the doctrine is an Indian one but the idea of a spiritual disconnect as time goes by exists in many traditions, and we are all familiar with the sense of nostalgia for a Golden Age in the distant past. This is the polar opposite to the modern belief in progress but does not necessarily conflict with it if we understand the traditional concept to relate to matters of spiritual consciousness and awareness of the source, while progress in the modern sense refers exclusively to the material world which includes the social, technological and political spheres. Of course, viewed from the spiritual standpoint, progress in these spheres is no progress at all if it derives from an ignorance of our true nature and results in a divorce between our material and spiritual selves. In fact, in this sense, it is the very opposite of real progress.

The beginning date of the Kali Yuga is interesting because it appears to coincide roughly with the start of recorded history. Thus, all that we regard as our known past falls within the period of spiritual ignorance, the lowest point in the cycle that runs from a pristine new beginning when men walk with the gods to the time when the gods withdraw, spirit is gradually obscured and our external physical environment becomes the principal focus of attention. Now, this may be a fall in one sense, it undoubtedly is a fall, but it is also a natural and inevitable occurrence that presumably has the purpose or effect of helping us develop aspects of our nature, primarily mental, that otherwise might remain in abeyance. How far it is taken, though, probably depends on us and our reaction to the cosmic winds of change. We can go completely with the flow of spiritual deterioration or we can recognise it for what it is and, to an extent at least, remain apart from it, staying centred in higher truth. The old saying that the stars incline but do not compel is relevant here.

The constituent parts of a full cycle are often referred to as Gold, Silver, Bronze and Iron (though this last, corresponding to the Kali Yuga, has nothing to do with the archaeological Iron Age when that metal. was first used), and, temporally, they stand to each other in the ratio 4, 3, 2 and 1. Thus, the Krita Yuga or Golden Age is four times longer than the Kali Yuga, which we can see from the dates above lasts for approximately five thousand years. So, the most recent Golden Age lasted for around twenty thousand years. Now, interestingly, because of the Law of Correspondences, each cycle can be broken down into mini cycles which exist in the same proportion and bear the same relation to each other as do the parts of the main cycle. So, within the Kali Yuga there are four sub-periods corresponding to Gold, Silver, Bronze and Iron which last for 4/10, 3/10, 2/10 and 1/10 respectively of the total duration. Remember the Kali Yuga in this system runs from 3102 BC to 2082 AD, so these sub-periods range from 2,076 years to 518 years, the period in which we find ourselves now, the tail end of the Kali Yuga. For ease of comprehension I'll put this in a table below in a form copied from Robert Bolton.

- Gold of Iron 3102 BC – 1026 BC 2,076 years
- Silver of Iron 1026 BC – 528 AD 1,554 years
- Bronze of Iron 528 AD – 1564 AD 1,036 years
- Iron of Iron 1564 AD – 2082 AD 518 years.

Those who wish, can look for patterns in these periods. They are not hard to find. The starting point coincides almost exactly with the beginning of ancient Egyptian civilisation, when King Menes united Upper and Lower Egypt and founded the First Dynasty. Modern historians place this to c. 3200–3030 BC. Robert Bolton points out that the second corresponds to the classical civilisations of Greece and Rome and the third to the Middle Ages. However, I want to break them down further by taking the last period and applying the same process to it. I want to do this for two reasons. Firstly, this period falls well within historical times and so events are more familiar to us, but secondly, there is the idea that as the cycles progress so time and the rate of change speed up. Therefore, the effects of cyclical change are easier to see. Once again, I am copying Robert Bolton with this table, whose fascinating book is the inspiration for this chapter. Please note that when it says 'Golden age' in the table what is meant is the first section of the fourth section of the Kali Yuga thus gold of iron of iron.

- Golden age 1564 – 1770 206 years
- Silver age 1770 – 1926 156 years
- Bronze age 1926 – 2030 104 years
- Iron age 2030 – 2082 52 years

It will be seen that we are now living in pretty grim times, spiritually speaking.

Looking at these dates, the first thing that strikes me is that the so-called Golden age of this sub-cycle went from the Reformation and the birth of science (as it is understood in modern terms) to the beginning of the Industrial Revolution. Galileo was born in 1564 and Beethoven in 1770. These are two individuals who can very well be taken as representing spirits of a new age. The one as a scientist who confronted religious authorities and the other as the most important artist of the

Romantic period, which was a definitive shift away from God as the centre to man as the centre. Whatever the quality of Beethoven's music might be, the fact is that it does signify a spiritual loss compared to what came before in that, the centre of Beethoven's music is Beethoven. In Romantic music the certainty of God is no longer present as it definitely was in Renaissance polyphony and even was in Baroque music. Man felt his exile from heaven more than ever before. It's probably a coincidence that the dates are so neat. We can't always expect things to fall into place quite so smoothly as this. The system is not an exact science and, despite all the dates given here, natural cycles are not arithmetically pure. Nevertheless, these dates do speak eloquently from a symbolical point of view, and when you add to them the fact that Francis Bacon, who is generally regarded as developing the modern scientific method, was born in 1561, and William Wordsworth, the foremost Romantic poet, was born in 1770, you have something quite impressive.

The Silver Age takes us right up to the brink of modernity. The 1st World War swept away the past, and the twenties are always regarded as the start of something quite new. Art, politics, everything, changed in ways too well known for me to need to set them forth here. So what I want to do now is break down the third period, the one in which we live and therefore, it could be said, the most important from our point of view. Please note that this time the golden age is the gold of bronze of iron of iron. I'm sorry – it's getting a little complicated at this point!

- Golden age 1926 – 1968 42 years
- Silver age 1968 – 1999 31 years
- Bronze age 1999 – 2020 21 years
- Iron age 2020 – 2030 10 years

The dates here are not quite exact because the periods do not break down into whole numbers precisely to the year, but they are near enough. The year 1968 is a significant date. It might be said to be when the momentum built up during the early sixties really kicked in and the new ways, a focus on youth, sexual liberation and so forth, spread from a select group right out to the whole populace. I believe it's when colour TV started in England and there's a whole symbolism right in that fact. Another significant year is 1999. Apart from being the end of the millennium, it can be seen as the time when computers and the internet started to enter every home. Of course, these things build up gradually, they don't come out of nowhere, but if you are looking for tipping points these dates are about the best there are.

You can carry on breaking these periods down endlessly. For instance, the bronze and iron ages of the period from 1926–1968 start around 1956 and 1964, which strike me as periods of significant change, while the silver age of the period from 1968–1999 coincides with the '80s, a time of increasing globalism, unregulated capitalism and the spread of what is known as cultural Marxism. Obviously, one can take this sort of thing too far but that does not discount the fact that, using this method, significant patterns emerge without them being forced to do so.

The question could nevertheless be asked, what is the point of all this? Is it just a bit of fun, the truth of which you can neither prove nor disprove, or does it have any purpose? To be honest, I'm not sure. I do think, though, that studying these dates can prepare us for change and help us to respond to it in a spiritually intelligent way. Particularly when you bear in mind that the dates are turning points, when what already exists for an elite or group of specialists spreads out into the mainstream. In 2020 we entered the next phase of the cycle and it is obvious that radical changes took place during that year, right on cue, you might say. As has occurred in previous stages, tendencies that had been building up over a period exploded dramatically into full manifestation. There won't be any going back. The final phase in the whole process comes in 2030. These may well be, to put it neutrally, interesting times, and it might help to know that there is some kind of pattern behind it all. Forewarned is forearmed. As those who remain loyal to God find the world crumbling around them, comfort can be found in understanding that this is more or less inevitable given the nature of things. But note that the fact of spiritual degeneration does not excuse those who go along with it or, worse, contribute to it for *"Offences must come but woe to that man by whom the offence comes"* (Matthew 18:7). Just because spiritual decline is naturally occurring in the world is no reason not to stand against it, especially since by doing so you may be able to mitigate its worst effects or help someone else struggling against it who might otherwise succumb. The situation is as it is, but you can make it better or worse. In a period of universal dissolution it makes little sense to try to preserve the past, but it is all the more essential to proclaim the truth.

The Modern Experiment

There is a school of thought that regards the whole development of modernity, beginning in the West in the Renaissance, as a terrible error, entirely destructive of true religion and spiritual understanding. I sympathise with that point of view but don't agree. The truth is, there was a great purpose behind what we loosely call the modern world but it was a risk that could either advance the human race and take it to new heights or else take it back to a primitive level from where it would have to effectively start again. Or even destroy it completely.

The experiment was in consciousness. Human consciousness became more focused on itself, more individual, so that it could be more creative and, once realigned to a spiritual sensibility, more godlike. From being largely passive children of God, we could become gods ourselves, able to wield divine powers for the creative enlargement of the universe. This was always intended as the evolutionary path that humanity should follow but in the West, a few hundred years ago, the process was stimulated and accelerated. A gradual evolution was boosted. This was done by the incarnation of certain highly evolved souls who could act like leaven in flour, obvious examples being the likes of Leonardo da Vinci, Shakespeare and Newton but there were many others at various levels and in various fields, and also, I would conjecture, by angelic forces acting on human consciousness from within. This double process has brought about the world today.

However, sound as the principles involved were, everything depended on the reception of human beings to their new powers, as powers is what they were. Would they use them to become more aware of God or would it be to pursue their own individual ends in their immediate environment? We know the answer to that. Does this mean the experiment has failed?

Not necessarily. It may be that it was never intended to be universal. Many individual souls have responded in a positive fashion. Many more (as is shown by the state of the world today) have not but if we think of comparisons in nature, this may be regarded as acceptable. For instance, how many seeds sprout and then grow to maturity? A fraction of those that are produced by the parent plants. This doesn't mean that souls that have not reacted properly, i.e. spiritually, are rejected and die, but they may be replanted in other environments more suitable to their state of evolution. That is what is happening now. It is a time of decision, a winnowing of souls, a real sheep and goats moment in the history of human evolution on this planet. This is probably why so many souls are alive now, to give as many as possible the opportunity to make a definitive spiritual choice.

Earth is like a field in which many seeds are sown. Generally, the growing process takes place in the normal course of events. Long periods go by when nothing much happens. Cycles roll round and there is little change. But sometimes growing conditions are enhanced, extra fertiliser is added, say, or there is an ideal combination of sun and rain. That is what has happened in the world, starting in the West and then, through the much maligned and misunderstood process of colonisation by the European powers, spreading elsewhere. Some plants have grown to be strong and upright, but others have either not grown as they should or developed in the wrong way and turned into weeds rather than beautiful flowers. Perhaps it depends on the original seeds, perhaps on how they have reacted for the peculiarity of these particular seeds is that their development is due to inner as well as outer factors. Now we are living at a time when the results of the experiment are being revealed. The stimulated individual consciousness of man is making its choice. A choice of God or self. The experiment is coming to an end. It was obviously not a full success. Indeed, it must be seen, as far as one can tell at the moment with limited vision, as a failure but then God knows what his intentions were and these may extend a lot further than we can see. (I say God. It is probably high spiritual beings more akin to the *elohim* of the Bible who are behind this experiment). But, as things appear to be here and now, the experiment has had only a limited success. The bulk of humanity has not responded to the stimulus in the right way. Perhaps, though, there will be either collectively or in the lives of each individual one final event that will call forth a definitive choice, a chance to put right errors of the past and seize the upward current. The groundwork is being laid with the diverging paths becoming more and more clearly marked out.

Divine sparks of consciousness come to Earth to unfold their innate qualities of Will, Love, Intelligence and Creativity. Incarnated in human bodies which have evolved as fit receptacles for them, they seek expression through the various groupings of mankind and epochs of history. They develop slowly. But each one of these sparks is individual and responds in an individual manner, even if this is not really perceived as such until a certain stage in the process is reached. At that stage, the process may be accelerated, pressures applied that will bring out innate qualities, good or bad. This is what has occurred over the last five centuries, though there are always greater cycles and lesser cycles so one cannot be completely dogmatic about this. But still one can say that the last half-millennium is highly unusual. One can also say that the momentum that started then is reaching its climax now. At one time there may have been the possibility of a great spiritual leap forward. That presumably was the hope. It seems certain that this hope will not be realised collectively but it certainly is still possible on an individual level.

The choice remains ours. To retune our individual self to the greater Overself of God or to keep it as a separate thing, pursuing its own limited ends in a limited material world. To join together in a holy marriage the two poles of spirit and matter within our being or to keep them separate, as in their different ways, the world-denying spiritual ascetic and the materialist do. Clearly, the ascetic is wiser than the materialist as spirit is the supreme principle but even he ignores the true divine destiny that is open to the modern consciousness in which goodness, beauty, truth and love can all be brought out into full expression.

* * *

It was the people of European ancestry who were behind this modern experiment. They had reached a sufficient stage of intelligence, creativity and sense of individual self to bring about a leap forward in consciousness. They were behind the art and science that built the new mind, which was a mind that could begin to interact with God in a positive sense. This is the real source of so-called 'white privilege'. It was an achievement unparalleled in the history of the world and advanced the human race considerably.

Unfortunately, it is now apparent that problems unavoidably built into the experiment, which might have been corrected and ironed out had they been addressed properly, have developed to the point at which they have derailed the whole thing. One cannot discount deliberate demonic intervention either, as these problems have been exacerbated by being encouraged. Atheism is foremost among them but there is also the perversion of the strong individual into the selfish egotist and the turning of innovation from creative, spiritually healthy channels to destructive and/or subversive ones. Give someone a box of matches. He can harness fire for useful purposes or he can burn the house down. We started to do the former, but we are now busily engaged in the latter. It would be nice to think we could come to our senses, but the process is clearly too far gone for that to happen.

The experiment has failed but has it failed completely?

I would say, no. The many benefits it brought about remain, certainly on higher levels of being where they have been built into human consciousness. And many individuals, probably many more than might be apparent from what we know, have moved on in their spiritual lives and developed the potential to approach God more closely than before. It may well be this was the real intention all along and that the collateral damage was expected. After all, we know that many are called but few are chosen. I am sure God knew exactly what he was about.

What is the School For?

We have said that Earth is a school for the evolution of consciousness, which is correct enough. But that is rather vague. One might also express its purpose as for the development of spirituality, a conscious, chosen, spiritual mind and attitude rather than the automatic, unchosen, passive one that exists in the higher worlds where the soul that eventually comes to Earth to further its education is formed. But that doesn't take us very far either. Spirituality can mean different things to different people, so let me try to define what I understand by the term.

First, though, we have to understand that the initial work has to do with the development of a strong individual self and mind. The soul cannot become an active, creative, intelligent, loving being, able to function as a spiritual adult, without that. It will remain something that is acted upon rather than acts. This formation of a true self explains much of the trajectory of human history over the past two thousand years but it should always have gone along with a spiritual outlook, as it did until relatively recently when the modern experiment began; a high risk experiment that could either have advanced the evolutionary process rapidly or else brought the whole thing crashing down.

What, then, is spirituality? This may seem a strange question to ask because the answer is surely obvious. Isn't spirituality just believing in a spiritual basis to life and then behaving in a way that corresponds to that? Well, yes it is, according to the simplest definition, but in reality spirituality has many sides to it, as you would expect if you are using a single word to describe the attitude of a Christ on the one hand and that of an ordinary believer, fully identified with his phenomenal self, on the other. Moreover, much that is called spirituality in our spiritual but not religious age is really just a kind of therapy or search for self-improvement, inner peace or what have you. There's nothing wrong with that but these things are not what the spiritual path is truly about.

I will attempt a few definitions here while stressing that it is all of these and more and cannot be limited to any single definition. But if we seek to lead a truly spiritual life then something of each of them should inform our approach to that end.

- *Spirituality is being true to your conscience.*

It is revealing that we all, believer or non-believer, saint and sinner alike, regard our conscience as representing something good to which we should adhere, and if we do not then we are falling short of some proper and objective standard. We might suppress the voice of conscience, but no one would claim that disobeying your conscience is an admirable thing or that it is a false friend which can potentially mislead. Conscience is an inner knowing that cannot be argued with and exists at a deeper level than thought or the pressure to conform to societal norms. It never suggests personal advantage which should tell us something about its source. At the same time, the reality of conscience does not mean that everything we might call conscience actually is such for we are multi-levelled creatures, not always able to recognise whence come our thoughts, feelings and ideas. Historically, many people have justified their opinions and actions as inspired by conscience or even God himself when a more objective view would show them to be heavily coloured by a personal ideology, if not prejudice. That is why my teachers told me **to be true to my conscience but make sure that it was my conscience I was being true to.**

- *Spirituality is a love of the laws of God.*

There are spiritual laws which are just as real as the physical ones we know about, more real, in fact, since the latter derive from the former, and these laws are the basis of creation and lie at the roots of our being. Real happiness and inner harmony can only come from observing them. They are presented in religions, though in forms appropriate to particular times and places, but can also be discerned in a pure form within one's own heart which is, as it were, stamped with truth, though the mind must be able to discern it there. And they are present in Nature even if it must be appreciated that this is a fallen world, so God's laws are by no means perfectly expressed in Nature as it exists on the physical level. My teachers told me that **there is nothing perfect in your world**, but there are echoes of perfection and signs pointing towards it, and we must be alert to these and able to discriminate between what is of God, hence of truth, and what is of fallen man or the human ego. God's laws are truth.

If you find the word law a little oppressive then be assured that the greatest law is love. But it is not the only one.

- *Spirituality is an awareness of the oneness of life.*

This is at once the easiest and most difficult thing to understand. It is almost a truism today to say that all life is one but who among us really lives as though that were the case? The oneness of life is a fact in consciousness for the saints but for the rest of us it is only a theory, albeit one we can, at least, try to live up to. Yet this oneness must be seen in the overall context of manifestation. All life is certainly one but in the created world there is a hierarchy of being which stretches from the highest archangel, who was one of the first thoughts of God, to the humble worker bee and below. Don't be put off by the word hierarchy, which has as its root meaning the sense of rule of the sacred. The sacred is the spiritual, and that which reveals more of pure spirit in its expression is always higher in the chain of being. My teachers said when speaking of beauty that it is **everywhere. It varies in degrees according to its closeness to God but there is God in everything**. In these words, we have the relation between the principles of hierarchy and oneness perfectly expressed.

- *Spirituality is awareness of the sacred.*

All life is sacred but see the quote above. I could rephrase it by saying that there is God in everything, but he is more revealed in some things than others. Awareness of the sacred is the ability to see this. When Christ was alive not everyone was able to recognize him for what he was. In fact, most people could not recognize him. Spirit has to be awakening in you for you to be able to perceive it in outer things. It is a sense of the sacred that first draws many onto the spiritual path. An awareness that a world without God is empty and dead. The sacred is that which is beyond quantity, and when it is denied the world is without meaning.

- *Spirituality is service, sacrifice and surrender.*

This is self-explanatory. It was a constant theme of my teachers who quickly disabused me of the idea that their presence had anything to do with my personal advancement. **Spiritual progress comes through service and sacrifice,** they said. This sounds rather fine in theory but when the reality of what it actually entails is made apparent, it is another matter. Plus, of course, the obvious point that if you think of any service and sacrifice you might be called upon to make as service and sacrifice that is exactly what they are not. They must be made willingly and almost joyfully if they are to be spiritually fruitful. As for surrender, this means letting go of everything remotely related to self and is really only possible for a saint. But then we have to become saints if we want to be spiritual, and there are no half measures in that. It is only by going through the fires of self-immolation that we can hope to become worthy of entry into the Kingdom of Heaven, which is what this school is all about.

- *Spirituality is observance of silence.*

I don't suppose there has ever been more outer stimulation to distract us from what is real. If we would discover the truth within, we have, at least some of the time, to withdraw our mind from attending to the constant stream of fast-moving images and the assault by ever more discordant sounds. There is also the noise of the mind itself that must be quietened. We have to get back to a more measured way of being and find a space in our lives for contemplation. Inner truths can only arise when the noise of the world dies away, and this noise is not just the buzz of the world's ceaseless activity but its very presence, for if the world is with us then we are with the world. Similarly, silence is not just an absence of sound but the womb in which awareness of that which lies behind the constantly shifting veils of form may be born. The modern technologically based world has made silence, not just auditory but mental too, very hard to find. Our technological dependence is one of the key factors behind our spiritual alienation.

- *Spirituality is simplicity.*

Many a time my teachers spoke to me of the need to be more simple and childlike. This did not mean that the mind should not be used and developed but that it should not be dominant. Thought divides and separates and that is good in the practical world, but we are called to a life in which the spiritual intuition is our basic guide and organ of knowing and perception. The intuition arises in simplicity. One comes to truth not through argument or analysis or debate but through direct seeing.

- *Spirituality is forgetting.*

It is forgetting your attachments and all the things that bind you to this world. Forgetting your frustrations and your fears, your desire to shine, to amass, to impress, to dominate and to control. From a certain point of view, not the only one but an important one, there is only one thing needful on the spiritual path, and that is to **forget the personal self** though note that this does not mean yourself as an individual. It is yourself as a separate individual divorced from God. We must see everything in the light of God even, especially, ourselves.

- *Spirituality is remembering.*

It is remembering what you really are and where you come from. It is remembering that this world is not ultimately real, certainly not in its current form. Most of all, the essence of spirituality is summed up in three simple words. **Remember the Creator.** Remember God and love him. From this love will come everything else. Without it there is no spirituality.

Two Approaches to the Spiritual Path

There are two main attitudes to the spiritual path, which can be roughly characterized as Eastern and Western, though neither way is exclusive to either hemisphere. The Eastern way, which can be summed up by Buddhism, is ahistorical. Truth is in pure being, a state of ego-less awareness in which the personal is transcended completely and all qualitative existence negated. Time is seen as illusion and the world of becoming, change, growth and development regarded as fundamentally unreal, even if it has a limited reality in its own sphere. This is the 'be here now' attitude, attained by complete detachment from everything in the world of creation. I realise that I am slightly caricaturing to make a point, but the essence of this approach is as described.

The Western way, summed up in Christianity, is historical. Life is moving on a path from incompletion to completion. The journey through the material world has a purpose, and matter itself with all that belongs to the created world, including, most importantly, the self, is not just discarded but gathered up, purified and then integrated with spirit in a holy matrimony. Being and becoming together are more than being alone and the evolutionary process, a historical thing operating in time, makes it possible. On this path, the good, the beautiful and the true are all valued, whereas in the former only the true has ultimate significance.

The difference between the two is not just in the relative importance given to time in the process but to the significance of the self. In the one, it is a veil on reality and an impediment to realisation. In the other, it is the whole point of the exercise, the means to spiritual fulfilment rather than the obstacle. And this implies that whereas enlightenment relates solely to eternity and so cannot be considered liable to further development, the

Christian idea of the purified self united with God is dynamic, capable of infinite development as the unfathomable depths of God are explored. For the Christian, time and the self are gathered up into spirit and sanctified.

Which brings us to the question of God. I take this as a baseline fact. God is. There is no debate to be had. If he were not, nothing would be. To the intellectual mind, this is evasive nonsense but the Creator of thought cannot be comprehended by thought. God is reality. Existence is spiritual. This cannot be proved intellectually but can be known on the intuitive level, which is where knowing and being are one. If God did not exist there would be no meaning and yet we know there is meaning or we would not be aware of its possibility nor feel the emptiness and horror of its absence.

But what form does God take? Is he impersonal reality as in the Buddhist conception or the Father as in Christian thought?

I have made the mistake in the past of equating God and the Absolute when I was under the fashionable misapprehension that all spiritual approaches said fundamentally the same thing and differences were largely down to expression. And that the mystics of all ages pointed to the same reality. I have also believed that the intellectual idea of the Absolute described something real. But I don't believe this anymore and, if truth be told, probably never really did, the confusion being more on a mental plane than a spiritual one.

What I mean is that God is not an abstraction but the most concrete, in the sense of most real, thing there is. The concept of the Absolute is the product of abstract speculation and is, in the striking words of Pascal, the god of the philosophers not of Abraham, Isaac and Jacob. The Absolute is being absorbed into non-being. It is thought taken to its limits and then, unable to go any further, postulating a theoretical void or emptiness beyond itself. It makes no difference if you call this a plenum-void as something is effectively swallowed up in nothing. The

Absolute is the result of a mode of cognition restricted to form trying to conceive of what lies beyond itself and coming up with something like dimensionless space, existence without being.

But God is not like that. The Absolute is existence as theory. God is existence as reality. He cannot be objectified as a thing. That is obviously true or he would be part of creation. He is not some thing. But he is not nothing either or even no-thing. He is the eternal Subject, the Great I AM, and note that in this statement the I comes before the AM. Person comes before being. There is no being without a Person to be. Abstract pure existence is a fantasy of the philosophers.

There may be no such thing as the absolute in the philosophical or even metaphysical sense but there is depth and there is mystery. Mystery is what exists beyond the limitations of the world as it is bound by space, time and form as normally conceived. It is the ground of freedom which is the essence of God and which he bestows on us in the form of our individuality. Mystery is also the source of creativity, which is God expressing himself in love. Love, creativity, freedom, these are real things and the true essence of God. The Absolute is really just an idea.

This doesn't mean that God can be comprehended. He may not be abstract being but he is transcendent and ultimate, the ground and source of everything, unlimited and eternal. But he is spirit, which means Subject not static impersonal being. And, as such, though he cannot be comprehended, he can certainly be known. This knowledge is communion which is the goal of the school. Spiritual communion entails three things which are two subjects and the relation between them. The subjects are the soul and God, and the relation is love.

Buddhism and Christianity

The two approaches to the spiritual path boil down to this. Is spirit ultimately personal or impersonal? Does life have a purpose and a goal or is it just a matter of seeing what it is? Is the ground of all things 'I' or just naked existence, a state of static universal oneness? To talk of a school necessarily implies purpose and goal. It also implies a headmaster who is behind the education process. And it means that the world is a creation, not something arbitrary or inexplicable. In each case the answer to the questions I have just posed is the first.

I have the greatest respect for Buddhism and for the Buddha himself, whose achievement was surely unparalleled in the purely human sense. However, Christ brought, indeed he was, a direct revelation from God which went beyond anything purely human.

What the Buddha taught and what Christ offers are two different things, even though there are substantial overlaps, and this should be understood at a time when many people believe all religions say essentially the same thing. Buddhism teaches the truth beyond the self, which the Buddha didn't actually deny but which he saw as obstructing spiritual realisation. For Christ, though, it is the self that is the ultimate means of reaching the state of union with God, a union that can be made more and more complete and ever fuller as that self develops in holiness. For the Buddhist, the self must be overcome completely but for the Christian it is sanctified, though that does require its overcoming as a self-centred or phenomenal thing.

The different attitudes to suffering bring out this distinction. The Buddhist seeks to escape suffering. That was the original motivation of Gautama, and a suffering Buddha makes no sense. He would be an unenlightened Buddha which is a contradiction in terms. The very definition of a Buddha is that he has gone beyond suffering. But Christ suffered, and for a Christian, suffering can be redemptive not merely a result of past karma as in Buddhism. And this shows us the difference between Christian love and Buddhist compassion. Love is fully personal, but compassion is universal, not really directed at one thing more than anything else and therefore, in a sense, impersonal. Because of this personal quality, love, even spiritual love, is vulnerable. It does not dwell on a lofty plane far removed from everyday reality. It is deeply involved in reality to the extent that it can fully feel the pain of reality.

Here are some questions I would put to a Buddhist. Do you accept that consciousness evolves? Or that life is purposeful? Do you have an explanation for creation? And if Buddhism maintains that we exist in relationship, that, as it puts it, all is interdependence, what is relating?

It seems to me that a person who becomes a Buddhist must suppress something within himself in order to do so properly. Note that Buddhism is essentially a monastic religion. What is suppressed is love in the personal sense but if love is not personal, what is it? As we saw, this is tied up with suffering. In the Christian story, Jesus suffered. Even God suffers, and that is because of love. In Buddhism suffering is what we need to escape from, what we need to free ourselves from. I know that in Mahayana Buddhism there is the figure of the Bodhisattva who renounces Nirvana until all sentient beings are released, but this suspiciously Christ-like figure is somewhat at odds with traditional Buddhist teaching and possibly came about because of the tendency to nihilism that contains within itself. I am not saying it is nihilistic but it can seem so. And the fact remains that if the individual is not real, if the person is not real, then love cannot exist. If the person is real, then God must be personal too, as the greater cannot come from the lesser. Later Buddhism tried to incorporate the virtues and values of the personal but had to be logically inconsistent with itself and its core teaching in order to do so.

Buddhism is unsurpassed in its insights and its development of 'skilful means' to overcome the ego and dis-identify with the phenomenal self. However, despite the later statement that Samsara (becoming) is not different to Nirvana (being), it cannot incorporate the full reality of creation into its vision of life. To say Samsara and Nirvana are one really means it's all Nirvana but actually diminishes the importance of the contribution and purpose of creation, which is to bring about a higher development in which reality becomes a relationship of multiple individuals united in love. This entails the marriage of created reality and uncreated being and brings about something new and more than the latter (the Nirvana state) on its own. Ultimately, the Buddhist rejection of God (and he is rejected because he is not fully accepted) turns out to be not its trump card, as often seen by modern people, but its Achilles heel. Reality is not impersonal oneness but fully and gloriously and eternally personal. And this is what Christianity teaches us more than any other spiritual approach. Having made that point, I should add that it does not invalidate the Buddhist approach. Before Christ came and redeemed the material world through his incarnation and self-sacrifice, it may have been the highest option. And even now there is an aspect of reality of divine oneness in which individual consciousness can be reabsorbed into the All with an end to participation in expressed being. But this is not the preferred option desired by God for his creation nor the reason for that creation in the first place, which was to make many gods existing together in a loving creative union in a constantly expanding spiritual universe.

The different approaches to reincarnation of East and West bring out this distinction with the Eastern view that it is a more or less endless cycle determined by karma (cause and effect) with no cumulative purpose other than to get off the wheel of rebirth through destroying the root of karma-making which is the self. The Western view is that it is a process of ongoing development leading to eventual attainment when evolution, should it progress as hoped, has brought about full growth and spiritual maturity. Again, the idea of goal and purpose through time.

Reincarnation

This is a subject that divides many serious spiritual thinkers. Some regard it as an integral part of the process that turns a man into a god. In the context of the school scenario of this book, each lifetime would be like a term before one went back to the spiritual world for the holidays. A number of the ancient Greeks, Pythagoras for example, believed in it. Others, however, see it as a mistaken doctrine. This would particularly be the case for most Christians and, as far as I know, all Muslims, both of whom took many of their founding beliefs from Judaism. Some of the early Christian Fathers, Origen for one, were believers in reincarnation but it was eventually decisively rejected by the church in favour of the idea that we have one life and one life only in which to earn our salvation. Here, I would like to set out why I believe in reincarnation, but also to add some caveats and provisos.

Let me start with a couple of relevant questions. What is man and what is his intended end? I see man, rather like his Maker, as triune. In other words, we are constituted of spirit, soul and body. Spirit is the uncreated part of us that is the spark of the divine fire within us. It is the point at which we and God intersect. The soul is our individual self. God is the spirit. God created the soul. But I don't think of the soul as the self we are aware of on an everyday basis. That is the soul as manifested in a body, our outer material form, the thing through which we experience the external world. By no means all the soul is consciously available to us 'down here'. It is a spiritual being and heavily restricted by operating through an earthbound brain and body. This gives rise to the ego, the sense of a separate self which is not so much an illusion, as some say, as an inevitable result of the constraints of being in a material, three-dimensional world. Put a spiritual being in a physical world and the ego is the result. We have to overcome that, or full identification with it, but the point is that it is a real thing; at least, it is so in terms of this world.

So, spirit, soul and body. That is what we are, simplified, certainly, but fundamentally this is how we are made up. And our intended end is to become consciously one with God. This requires the union of the soul, the individual self, with spirit, the universal self or God. Consciously one. Spirit on its own level is one with God but not consciously so, not in an individual sense. You might well ask why God wants to create individuals. He is God, surely all-sufficient in himself? No doubt that is so but it leaves out two important factors. One, God is creative. His nature is self-expression and abundance, becoming more. He becomes more through other beings, some of whom are us. And two, God is love. What does love want to do? To give of itself and to have a relationship with the loved one. Again, that is us. That is why God creates us as individuals with free will. What kind of relationship can you have with slaves and automata?

Thus far I have said nothing with which a non-believer in reincarnation would necessarily disagree. The question now is what is the process by which a newly created soul becomes a god? I think it requires experience in the material world, which is the place where separation is possible and the inner and the outer are most differentiated. Through the sense of being separate we can develop our individual self, which we must do before we can consciously transcend it in union with God. This all has to be done as a free and conscious act. I would accept that certain forms of learning can take place in non-material spheres of existence but this world is the best environment for an undeveloped soul to grow into self-awareness and eventually grow out of self-awareness, because it is the place in which the soul is alone. It's where the soul can suffer and where it can learn from that and move on to a new and higher level of understanding and self-mastery. And it takes a lot more than one life for a soul to progress from a more or less unconscious oneness with nature (its environment), which is the condition of primitive man, to a fully conscious union with God which would include all of life. In the process, the same soul develops the faculties of will, intelligence and love, all dependent on self-consciousness and none really known to primitive man to any serious degree.

That's the theory. From a personal perspective, I believe in reincarnation for several reasons. Intellectually, it makes sense for the reasons given above. The idea that human beings, so individual and so different, with widely varying talents and destinies, came into being with physical birth seems far-fetched to me, but I realise that a doctrine of pre-mortal existence could account for that. Speaking of which, I never had any doubt that I had existed before my birth in this world. As a child I had dim memories of higher worlds (Wordsworth's clouds of glories) and though they inevitably faded, they left an indelible mark on my consciousness. Then, as I grew older certain historical periods and cultures seemed very familiar to me. That proves nothing, I know, but was personally convincing. Added to these personal impressions there is also the fact that when I encountered the Masters (see appendix) they made certain comments that strongly implied reincarnation. For instance, that I had asked to come back to this world. I was further told that their medium and I had been together in the past and that I had a previous connection with India. They referred on one occasion to my **karmic weakness** (karma being the consequences of one life manifesting in another) and said a tendency to mental sluggishness (undeniably true, alas) was **partly due to karma.**

Now, this might mean that I have had previous lives here but not everyone has but I don't incline to that interpretation for the reason given above; that this world is the best arena for learning particular lessons and that it takes a very long time to turn a primitive man into a saint.

Reincarnation is rejected by Christianity, but it could have

been one of the many more things that Jesus wanted to say to
his disciples which they could not currently bear (John 16:12).
It's also possible that as a belief in only one life might give one
a much greater impetus to seek salvation in that life, it was not
taught in the religion destined for the West. We know how certain
parts of the world that do believe in reincarnation tend to view
life in terms of endless cycles and even to fall into stagnation.
It may be that the part that was intended to be more spiritually
dynamic and creative, that was the first to see life in terms of
historical progression, had the idea of reincarnation removed to
encourage a different type of consciousness, one that was more
independent, innovative and outward looking. And, after all,
belief in reincarnation has no particular relevance in the context
of treading the spiritual path, so its omission is not important in
that respect. So, I don't think the fact of Christianity's rejection
of reincarnation is that significant. There are hints of it in the
Bible and, though these are often explained away, I would say
that as long as scripture, by which I chiefly mean the teachings
of Jesus in the Gospels, doesn't deny it outright, a Christian can
have an open mind on the subject.

This is the basis of my belief in reincarnation. At the
same time, I would add that, while reincarnation may have
explanatory power for the inequality of men, why some suffer
and some are rich and others not and so on, it is not something
to pay too much attention to in this world. Undue interest in
searching out details of past lives will only distract you from
the here and now, the lessons you have to learn today. All you
need to know about your past is in you now, in the present time,
in your character, your tendencies, your weaknesses and your
strengths. It doesn't matter if you were a notable person in the
16th century. Now you are who you are today and that is all you
should focus on if you are to learn what you are supposed to.

Why don't we remember previous lives? If reincarnation
is true how is it that no one (to all intents and purposes) can

remember their past incarnations in this world? I don't see this as a problem. The doctrine is not saying that I, William Wildblood, existed in a previous life in such and such a place at such and such a time. It is saying that the soul that took birth as WW in this life took birth on a former occasion, but then it manifested through a different mind as well as a different body. The brain on each occasion was entirely a new thing, though the form the mind that used that brain took would have been decided by causes originating in the past and determined by karma (see above) and the needs of that particular lifetime. So, WW is a new person in this life, though he is not just made from his parents' genetic material. His karma, his purpose and the quality of his soul all play a part in making him what he is. As mentioned earlier, my teachers told me, and this is something I also feel, that **the greater part of you remains with us**. That is the soul, of which only a fraction manifests through the earthbound personality. May I reassure those who think this means that when a loved one dies you will never meet them again in the form you knew that this is not the case. They will be more truly themselves, just as you will be. The real individual will stand forth, almost as though a limited being acquires an extra dimension.

If and when reincarnation becomes more established as a concept in the West, it should not be viewed in the same way as it was, and generally still is, in the East. For a start, the idea that human beings can be reborn in animal form should not be a part of it. It is not impossible, I suppose, that extreme karma might cause a man to be born as an animal. However, at this stage of human evolution, meaning the unfolding of the spiritual seed within, that would be a vanishingly rare event. The point of reincarnation is education not punishment and, though painful conditions might sometimes be necessary, they only come about in order to teach a soul what it needs to learn. Then there is the idea of the soul or higher self as the reincarnating agent, which is not properly present in Hinduism or Buddhism. There is no real individual in Buddhism, of course, and the *jiva* in Hinduism appears mostly to be just an individual unit of consciousness with none of the sense of a higher self or **greater part of you** that I would give it. So, I would hope that Western ideas of reincarnation would view souls as real spiritual beings, with a real life on their own spiritual plane, who come to this Earth to learn needed lessons before returning to what is their real home. That home is not their final destination but it is still their current real home, the place they originated in as souls and where they belong for now. The experience of reincarnating in this world is designed to take them deeper into the heart of God and to transcend their limited individuality in divine oneness, but that is for the future. Now, they have a home and it is in the spiritual realm not the physical plane of this Earth. So, what I am saying is that reincarnation is better viewed from the standpoint of the higher self or soul than that of the man as he is on this Earth. It is the soul that takes incarnation, rather than the man who has been incarnated, that is the important element in all this.

For any spiritual believer there are three possibilities of our whereabouts before we were born into this world. Firstly, we were nowhere and it's an entirely new person. This is what materialists would say and it's also what most orthodox Western religions teach. For me, it's the least plausible of the options. It really doesn't take into account the vast differences between human beings and their lives in this world, never mind the intuition that some people have that they are not beginners at the game of life. Then there is the idea of pre-mortal existence. We may not have been in this world before, but we have not come from nowhere. Our creation was in a spiritual realm and we have lived and learned in higher worlds before coming to this one. This makes much more sense than a fresh creation but, for me, it still doesn't provide as satisfying an answer as reincarnation. I certainly agree that there is a pre-mortal or pre-physical existence which is that of the soul on its own level or other non-material levels but I think earthly experience is required on many occasions before one has extracted all the possibilities this world has to offer and learned all it has to teach. But that's just my belief. No doubt we shall only find out for certain when all mysteries are revealed in the fullness of time. Until then the important thing is to love and serve and seek to know our Creator to the best of our ability.

Some Objections to Reincarnation

Although reincarnation is not part of orthodox Christian belief, I don't see it as conflicting with the essential message of Christ. Many Christians, however, do have objections to it and I will consider a few of those here.

1. It does away with the need to acquire salvation in this life now.

If reincarnation is true do we all get chance after chance until we get it right? Is that reasonable? Doesn't it provide an excuse to sin? Why bother making spiritual efforts if everything will come good in the end anyway?

My response to this is that perhaps we do get many chances to 'get it right'. After all, if we are enjoined to forgive those who slight us 70 x 7 times, then would we not expect God to extend the same consideration to us when we fail or fall short? It would be strange if he told us to do one thing and did another himself. Having said that, it should be understood that the way we fail or fall short will determine the circumstances of our life next time round. All belief systems which include reincarnation also have reaping what you sow at their heart. So, there's no excuse to sin, and wrongdoing will always bring about consequences.

However, I would add the important proviso that it is unlikely that the granting of new chances lasts forever. There may come a time when we have used up our opportunities, and if a soul wholly rejects God rather than simply fails to accept him then that rejection could be taken as decisive. Therefore, while a state analogous to the traditional concept of hell probably does exist, it is not necessarily permanent except in the case of those who through pride, defiance, or whatever it may be, voluntarily choose spiritual extinction rather than God. And even they are given what they want.

Thus, while not discounting the real possibility of damnation for some souls who persistently defy and deny God, it seems improbable that most non-believers are bad enough to go to hell eternally. Think of people you know who don't believe in God, perhaps among them friends and family. Would you give them another chance? Then why not God? He presumably wants to bring as many of his children back to him as possible and would always incline more to mercy than justice, though the demands of justice will still have to be met.

But there is another point. Reincarnation is not chiefly to do with the process of salvation or damnation but with that of spiritual development. This means it concerns the theosis or god-making side of the equation. So, it may be that there are two things going on when we come to this world. One, the requirement to turn away from self and towards God, and two, the learning of lessons that will eventually convert us into saints. After all, most of those who might technically be saved are still a very long way from sainthood and, while not disputing the role of purgatory in the afterlife, it seems clear that experience in the material world is also necessary for the long and slow process of transforming a standard model human being into a saint. Only here are certain temptations, tests and growth scenarios possible. Only here can certain challenges be met, and it is through overcoming these challenges that latent virtues can develop.

2. Christians object to reincarnation on the grounds that it conflicts with the idea of the resurrection of the body.

Does it? What exactly is the body anyway? When we reincarnate, we clearly do not have the same body we had before but the one we do have is the product of the earlier one. It is refined or degraded to the degree that earlier body was refined or degraded. We carry our past with us in the present and that is true for the body, too, which may be built on hereditary principles but also has the imprint of the soul within the limits imposed by the restrictions of karma or our destiny for that life. My belief is that eventually the atoms of our physical body will be transmuted into light and that the resurrected and ascended spiritual body is not a flesh and blood thing but a body of light. Again, the reincarnation process gradually burns away the dross in the body that prevents its transmutation, and the body we eventually acquire, or build, is the product of many lives of purification and refinement.

3. Another objection is that reincarnation implies an unnatural separation between body and soul, making them two wholly different things.

But they clearly are two different things. The human soul can exist without a body, certainly without a physical body, though it probably always has a form of some kind. A physical body enables it to experience life in the physical world and, though I do believe it is certainly part of what we are, it is not this body that matters but 'bodyliness'. The body of the elect is not physical though there is probably something in it which corresponds to transmuted matter. Reincarnation certainly implies the pre-existence of the soul before it acquires a body, but it is not saying that spirit is good and matter bad as some of the Gnostics did. It merely points to the fact that we are primarily spiritual beings.

4. Why can we not remember our previous lives?

This one is easy to answer, but first I would say that if we actually could remember past lives we would hardly be able to learn anything new in this one. Memory is often a burden and prevents us living in the present moment, and that's just the memories of a single life. Imagine if we had a whole series to recollect. But, more to the point, we cannot remember our previous lives because we, as who we are now, do not have any previous lives. This is our first and only life. For it is the soul that comes and goes, not the person we are now.

To appreciate this requires an understanding of what you might call esoteric anatomy, which posits a higher self or soul that exists on its own spiritual plane and sends down a portion of itself to experience life in this world. So, the mind, emotional nature and sense of personal identity are as new as the physical body, though based on what has gone before. It's a crude analogy but imagine the soul on a higher plane as a sun sending down a shaft of light (its consciousness) through mental, emotional and physical levels, and clothing itself with a 'body' of each one in order to function on that level. These are all new and it is with these that we normally identify and think of as ourselves. The directing soul is, as it were, hidden, except in rare moments, even though it is the animating principle of the whole thing and, to an extent, defines its quality. I have mentioned the Masters' words that **the greater part of you remains with us**. The being you are in this world is only a part of the totality of what you really are, though how much a part depends from individual to individual.

I have looked at a few Christian objections to reincarnation here, but it may be that conventional Christianity has an incomplete understanding of the reason for our being in this world when it focuses on salvation rather than theosis. Salvation is certainly important. Souls that reject God have proved they are not worthy of him. Life in this world, where such a rejection is possible, has brought out and proved their innate tendencies and they have excluded themselves from the higher life. But the governing idea behind the theory of reincarnation in its Western form is that individual units of consciousness, souls, need to experience life in this world over many occasions in order to evolve their consciousness. Newly made by God as sparks from the central fire of his own being, they are intended to grow to godlike status themselves by becoming fully aware of the spiritual reality of their own being as given by God. Reincarnation with its opportunities for experience and expression is the process that brings this about. That's the theory anyway, though whether it applies to everyone in this world or is only one of various methods of spiritual growth is another matter.

End Times and Reincarnation

Can anyone doubt that these are the End Times as spoken of in the Christian tradition? Almost everywhere materialism and atheism have triumphed, and where spirituality does exist it is often a weak, impoverished thing that takes more of its ideology from contemporary political thought than religious teaching. Most people in the West reject Christianity and, of those that do embrace it, many see it in the light of the secular humanism that has developed since the 18th century. Christianity, it is thought, must be revised to reflect that rather than that being seen as wholly secondary to the Christian vision. I believe that traditional Christianity does need to be looked at afresh from the perspective of a developing consciousness which sees humanity as growing into godhood but this should be done by deepening it not by making it spiritually shallow, which is what is actually happening. The heart of Christianity is neglected, and teachings that only really apply to those who have renounced the sins of the world are opened up to all regardless of repentance. That, at least, is becoming the popular conception of the real meaning of the Christian message. God loves everybody equally, it is claimed, irrespective of what they are or how they behave. No doubt God does love all his children, but he loves truth, too, and if you love him, you keep his commandments. Only then can his love be expressed without the other side to it, which is his anger, considering anger as a metaphysical aspect of justice. For justice and mercy must always go together.

To imagine that God loves everyone equally, regardless of the degree to which they reflect his own reality back to him through their own love, is to misunderstand what this world and its purpose are for. It is a testing ground for souls to see which ones, when separated from inner truth, still incline towards that holy reality, and which do not but seek the furtherance of the ego. Again, you could put the matter like this. Who responds primarily to the pull of spirit and who to that of matter? God loves those most who love him because they are his true children, not just born of him as all are, but like him. To say that God loves everyone equally reduces love to a quantitative thing, very appropriate for our materialistic time. But spiritual love is above all qualitative because it is personal.

There is this idea of unconditional love, which is presumably born of the true fact that God is love; love is his nature, expressed from his heart as rays from the sun, shining on the good and bad alike. But here's a question. If God loves everything unconditionally, does he then love evil?

Obviously not. God loves something because it is. Existence is good. It comes from him and it is him. But a creature's free will can deform that goodness into evil. God still loves the creature for the goodness that is inherent in the fact of its existence but he does not love the form in which it has chosen to express itself and the more it identifies with that form, the more it separates itself from him. God's love is always there but it has been rejected and that rejection is fundamentally an act of hatred. God does not love hatred. How can you love hatred since hatred is the denial of love? How can you love evil since evil is the rejection of good and love is the recognition of good? God is not beyond good and evil as the popular fallacy has it. In God there is only good. Evil is the refusal of God. It is the shadow cast by good in a world in which good must be consciously chosen.

Does God love a saint more than a sinner? Yes, he does, for he only loves the good and in the saint there is both existential good and expressed good while in the sinner there is only the former. God still loves the sinner because of his existential good but while the saint is shining God's light back to him, the sinner has put up a dark barrier that kills that light The saint reflects God but the sinner rejects him. God does not love sin because it is the denial of his own reality which is truth but he loves the sinner which is why he sent his Son to the world. If he loved the sinner for himself *qua* sinner, as he loves the saint for himself, he would not have needed to do this. Christ would not have been necessary. But Christ was necessary. Christ shows that God does not love evil. He only loves the good.

* * *

I've gone slightly off the point I wish to address in this chapter. What I have just written is not without relevance to the subject, but I am jumping ahead of myself. I want here to try to reconcile a belief in reincarnation with the idea of judgment. That's because both form part of my understanding of the spiritual world and, at first sight, they seem contradictory. Reincarnation is normally assumed to mean you have an unspecified number of lifetimes to get it right. You live a life and learn or don't learn and in your next life you carry on from where you have left off in a new incarnation, the circumstances of which will be a result of the previous one or the previous ones. The consequences of mistakes will be experienced in a future life, and you evolve, you develop, gradually growing into higher consciousness. That's the theory which is appealing to many because it has a certain logic to it.

However, I don't think things are that simple. Today's world is radically different to previous eras for many reasons ranging from a hugely expanded population, to great material comfort and technological sophistication, to access to all the wisdom of the past for anyone who cares to look for it, to the decay of all forms of religion. It is a time of crisis and I believe many people are being born now to experience a world in which a definitive choice has to be made between good and evil, truth and lies, with the latter often being presented as the former, which makes it a real test of one's inner compass and true orientation. And also, of courage. For it does take a certain amount of courage to hold onto one's faith in the true God when so many false alternatives are being presented, usually with the assumption that they are more intelligent, more compassionate or just that to hold them is the sign of a good person. We will find as time goes on that to stand by real Christian values will be seen as the mark of an ignorant or even bad person. That is because these values put God above Man. Modern ideology cannot countenance that. God, if he exists, must adapt himself to human requirements, and his purpose for us must involve the increase of happiness and concomitant decrease of suffering in this world.

Might it be that the population of the world is currently at an all-time high because so many souls are being assembled for a comprehensive test of their spiritual quality and dedication? Circumstances are being made hard in order to sort out the spiritual sheep from the goats. Now is an important time of decision when humanity will be divided into those who make the spiritual grade and those who don't, with the failures (which may be a hard word but is accurate) being sent elsewhere to learn the lessons they refused here. Where that elsewhere will be and what its nature will consist of, I cannot say but I would guess that it will be a descent into a lower level of consciousness which will require a concerted effort to escape from. There will be increased separation from the source with fewer of the consoling worldly pleasures one can find here.

This is how I reconcile reincarnation and judgment. During the course of a world age souls incarnate at various times and in various places with the aim of developing spiritual consciousness, which requires for its proper growth the full sense of duality and awareness of individuality. Only by becoming a fully aware self can the God-created individualised spark of spirit grow into godhood and become a co-creator in the fullness of life, which is God's wish for us. If we stayed in the heavenly realms without incarnation, we would remain spiritual babes. Independence is acquired through incarnation.

But a world age comes to an end and that is what ours is now doing. It's the end of school, the time when all spiritual students must take their exam to see if they can pass on to the next stage. Call it graduation. Those who succeed, on whatever level, because some are primary school students while others are at higher stages, ready for full graduation into theosis, ascend to higher levels appropriate to their consciousness. Those that do not pass this spiritual exam descend. The choice is ours and it is never too late to make the decision that will be determining. There are temptations galore at the moment, precisely to test the heart. They range from simple materialism and atheism to numerous false forms of spirituality, united in their focus on the human self and its spiritual potential independent of God. But it is up to us to see through all of these and open our hearts and minds up to the true reality of God. Then we must act on the measure of that reality without distorting it by egotism, emotionalism or pride. In this we are most guided by dedication to the person of Christ who is the human representation of God. The truth of his being will direct us to the truth of our own being. Using him as a kind of universal standard time by which we set our own spiritual clocks will serve us well when the moment comes for the judgment of our soul.

What is Evolution?

We have come a long way since we began our schooling on planet Earth. We have left behind our spiritual childhood of instinctive union with nature and moved out of that infantile condition, separating ourselves from the natural world which we have then sought to dominate and bring under our control. This was all right and proper in context and helped us develop our innate will and intelligence, two things strongly associated with the sense of self. And this is precisely what we have been doing, developing our sense of an individual self. Early man either did not have this at all or else had it in a very limited way. His consciousness would have been tribal before it was individual.

So, we have made substantial progress on our evolutionary journey and are now right in the stage of separation which is the result of our focus on self. But here is the problem. We should have moved on from this some time ago. We should have started to re-embrace a spiritual worldview and begin the journey back upwards, envisioning this journey in the form of a U where the top left is the start of the journey, the bottom is our current position and the top right is spiritual completion.

We should have done this, but we haven't. We have got stuck in what some people describe as a case of arrested adolescence. Since we are basically rebelling against our Creator, our Father, and asserting ourselves and our independence, that is a good description. The rejection of tradition, the sexual revolution, the all-pervasive leftism, the concern with image and the attempts by the old to emulate the young all point to the same conclusion of spiritual immaturity.

In all its details this process is extremely subtle and complicated but fundamentally it is very simple. God creates human beings as individual souls with free will. If you are going to be individual, you must be free and vice versa, and this fact of freedom is the most profound thing that points ineluctably to a spiritual origin. There can never be freedom in a purely material world. The fact of freedom also tells us that this is a real creation not a semblance of such as postulated in some metaphysical approaches. God gives human souls part of himself, his own reality and his own freedom and we share in his being even to the extent of being potential little gods ourselves. His children, in fact. God does this for two reasons. One, his nature is love so he wants to share, to give. And two, so that his creation may be more interesting to him. Imagine a creation that runs like clockwork. Pretty dull really. But imagine if you create something which has the potential to create itself from within. Then you can observe the results which might be surprising even to you, the original creator. Of course, this is crudely expressed and might appear to ignore the fact (I don't think it does really) that God sees the whole of time now, in this very moment, but it does, I believe, cover something of God's purpose in creation.

We start as new-born spiritual babes, one with our environment and not consciously separated out from that. But then, as we grow and start to explore and experience the world, we become more aware of ourselves as the inner subject. As time goes by, the inner subject dominates our consciousness more than the outer object though our lives exist as an interaction between the two. But eventually we become wholly identified with the inner subject, and this results in a sense of alienation which is quite clearly our current position. It's the bottom of the evolutionary arc. Now is the time to ascend, to go back to the understanding and realisation that we are one with life and to become full participants in the wholeness of being but this time in an active, conscious mode which includes creativity and will. Thus, atavistic attempts to revert to the securities of spiritual childhood whether that be in the form of fundamentalist religion or neo-paganism, along with a whole host of other manifestations of escapism, are not what is required. Fundamentalist religion is literalistic in that it mistakes concrete symbol for spiritual reality or outer form for inner truth. It does not require its practitioner to be spiritually creative or develop intuitive insight, which is the primary spiritual task of the present day. Neo-paganism is a modern concoction deriving from a mixture of nature worship and 20th century occultism. It refers itself to the creation not the Creator and has no proper sense of the transcendent or understanding of Christ. In a way, both these attitudes to the spiritual path are materialistic. They are certainly indicative of a worldly mind's approach to the spiritual because they interpret it in the context of that mind.

The solution is to grow up spiritually, which we do by accepting the transcendent dimension of life and then seeking to attune ourselves to it though a conscious attempt to think and to know according to its reality. We move from the Adamic state of passive oneness with life or nature to a self-consciousness in which the sense of separation is primary, but that means that freedom can start to be known and self will developed. That, in turn, leads to the prison of the self-enclosed ego. We have to break out of that, and the only way is to seek our true being in God. Not in the sense of being absorbed by him. The aim is to become conscious partners with God in an ever-expanding celebration of creation. Not equal partners, of course, but joined in a relationship of oneness in love.

So much for the path to be trodden; but how, practically speaking, do we tread it? The key to it all is in Christ. He was the forerunner who showed us the way, but he is also, as he said, himself the Way. It is through him that the path is trodden. He cannot be set aside or even regarded as one way amongst many. He is the Way and the Goal. To recognise this is the first step but the recognition must be constantly deepened until Christ is actually born in the heart and you start to become him. This is still an initial phase. The infant Christ must grow, mature and develop before he can 'go to the Father' and be made fully one with him. This stage is where natural processes of evolution are superseded, and the work must become conscious, which explains why our development has stalled. We have not been able to make the transition from beings passively acted on by evolutionary forces to consciously co-operating participants in our own spiritual expansion.

* * *

The doctrine of the Kali Yuga alluded to earlier, in the Cycle of Changes chapter, might seem to conflict with the idea of spiritual evolution. After all, if the spiritual state of humanity was at a higher level thousands of years ago, how have we evolved? But that is to confuse an objective state with a subjective one. The spiritual condition and environment were purer thousands of years ago, but the personal achieved spiritual level of individuals was not. There were not a host of saints and sages walking around, though there may well have been some. There may also have been those who have come down to us in myth described as gods but these would have been beings from higher levels come to teach infant humanity. We had to descend from a higher state of environmental spirituality to fully experience material conditions but then we must rise again, this time as fully conscious individuals with our own in-built spiritual awareness that is not dependent on outer circumstances. This is evolution.

Progress vs Evolution

We need to distinguish between three quite different things: spiritual evolution, evolution considered in Darwinian biological terms, and progress, conventionally understood. It is only the first that is relevant to the earth as school scenario. Evolution as in random mutation and natural selection is certainly a means whereby the proliferation of forms exist in the world, though it is a mistake to take it as the sole means. There are also spiritual forces working to determine how life expresses itself but, given the element of freedom in creation, natural selection is undoubtedly part of the process of evolving life forms. Remember, though, that the significant evolution is on the level of consciousness and the forms exist as the most effective mediums through which that evolution may take place. We are only concerned in this book with human evolution, but it should be apparent that the whole of the natural world is undergoing its own form of growth and development. Life, wherever it is and however it manifests, is always in the process of becoming more. Here is the reality behind the controversial doctrine of endless economic growth. It does have some basis in truth but is just applied to the wrong level, material rather than spiritual.

Evolution is different to progress, which is a secular version of messianic Christianity. Partially so, at least. It derives at various removes from the eschatological idea of the coming of the Kingdom of God on the one hand, and Darwinian evolution on the other. It is conceived as a continuing move forwards into more enlightened times, supported by, indeed possibly totally dependent on, new technology. It doesn't really make any sense from a materialistic point of view, since everything in materialism is without meaning or purpose, but the idea is that human beings can create their own purpose after a certain point and build on that. What the values driving it are and where they come from don't seem to be deeply considered and this is where assumptions derived from Christianity come in, but these sit squarely on the reality of God so there is a contradiction which is not addressed. But never mind.

Progress, as we understand it now, essentially means everything will get better. Everyone will be happier, and suffering will be reduced. Putting it in those terms, it should be obvious what a superficial idea it is, and that's before you even look at how things are working out in the world. What is more, one man's progress might well be another man's headlong rush into collapse. For example, is feminism progress? It certainly is from the modern liberal perspective, but not from a traditional conservative one which values the time-honoured different and complementary roles of the two sexes, seeing these as based on cosmic law. Does that mean we must call the traditionalist regressive? Then you are defining progress in terms of how one group sees it and you are essentially making it political. You can call that moral if you like but you would be deceiving yourself. It is entirely political as is further borne out by the fact that the concept of historical progress is heavily linked to the French Revolution and Marxism, two of the most anti-spiritual and political events and attitudes of the last couple of centuries.

The idea of progress is a materialistic perversion of the true fact of spiritual evolution. It brings down to the horizontal plane something that functions spiritually. But spiritual evolution does not necessarily mean material progress. Sometimes, in the past, it has done so but it is increasingly less likely to as we take our focus of attention off the world as it is in and for itself and start to see it in its true light as a Creation and only a temporary home. This will not lessen our love and respect for it. Quite the reverse, in fact. It is part of God's universe, so we will treasure it and honour it in that capacity, but we will not make either it or the earthly part of our being the primary focus of our attention.

In future it will be seen that creation and evolution are two sides of the one coin. Once we understand that this world is a creation then we will see that creation is meaningless without evolution. That is its purpose. Viewed from such a perspective, the Genesis story takes on a slightly different meaning. God did not put Adam and Eve in the Garden of Eden expecting them to stay in the same state forever. They were supposed to grow and become more aware of themselves and of him. Their sin was in trying to force growth from the point of view of the grasping ego rather than letting it happen naturally. (A similar sin, incidentally, to that of those who seek heaven through drugs). So, the Fall was a genuine Fall. Things were not intended to happen like that, and ultimately, the situation could only be put right by the incarnation of Christ who redeemed corrupted matter, which meant that the spiritual path could now include the whole of creation rather than seek to leave the fallen, material world behind for entry into spirit alone, as in the Buddhist way. The Fall led to suffering and death and meant that evolution became hard, but it was not, as is sometimes speculated, a necessary event without which we would have remained spiritual infants. It resulted in full separation from God and the consequent birth of the ego but one can envisage a different scenario in which evolution unfolded more naturally and inevitably, rather than what we have now where it is neither natural nor inevitable and involves sin and suffering.

I reject the idea of secular progress which amounts to little more than the deification of reason. Reason is an excellent tool but makes a very poor god. It doesn't even know where it comes from. But I would also point out that as new secularised societies form, hoping to improve on past ones, they always have new evils accompanying them, either the defects of their qualities (to put it kindly) or unacknowledged spiritual sins which are the consequence of their ideological structure, assumptions, prejudices and oversights. The best you could say about them is that while they may offer some improvements in certain areas, they bring about radical decline in others. Our own modern society, which is the most spiritually illiterate one to be known in the West so far, is a perfect case in point.

On the other hand, spiritual progress is what the school was built to bring about. Though by no means inevitable because of the inviolable law of human freedom, it is possible should we wish to avail ourselves of the learning opportunities we are given in this world. Our individual progress depends on ourselves as pupils, just as in ordinary life. Whether this individual progress translates to societal progress is a difficult question. Sometimes it might, sometimes it might not, all depending on the stage in any particular cycle – see the Cycles of Change chapter. Today you might even say that greater spiritual progress on an individual level can be made because of the lack of general spiritual awareness. If we can identify this and resist it then we build truth into our soul and make it our own more effectively than if we were just following the crowd in a spiritually benign era.

There is one other rather important difference between progress considered as spiritual development and the materialised, secular version. Spiritual progress has a goal and an end. It leads to union with God and, in terms of the Christian myth, the establishment of the New Jerusalem. I am not so much interested in the literal truth of this idea as in the sense it encapsulates of divine purpose and fulfilment. We are not just proceeding on a never-ending path going who knows where, in fact not going anywhere, just going ceaselessly onwards. We have a destiny, there is a plan and a journey's end where all is consummated, and we enter into glory. Time is not meaningless endless change but the means whereby we arrive at eternal life which will be a state, unimaginable to us now, in which time and eternity both exist, the former transfigured and, like matter, itself raised up into spirit. Time can either continue forever in dreary monotony or end in nothingness or be completed in eternity where it will not die but be transformed. This last is the goal towards which spiritual evolution is working.

Death

Death is the meaning of life. At least, properly understood it is. Misunderstood, it shows the meaninglessness of life being the return of existence to non-existence, which makes existence more or less pointless. But seen as the moment at which material life returns to spiritual it puts earthly life into perspective, giving it purpose. Imagine life without death. That really would be terrifying in its banality, even if it included eternal youth.

At one time, early on in my spiritual journey, I read some of the spiritualist literature. While interesting and optimistic about the afterlife, it was always slightly unsatisfactory because so much of the life described seemed too much like the better aspects of this life stripped of pain. I realise this would be what is called Summerlands and that spiritualism posits higher levels of reality above that, but even so there was always an element of the mundane and expected about the whole spiritualist description of the post-mortem world. I am not denigrating it because I do believe it gave something that blind faith didn't to millions, at a time when people were reaching out for something more, but it never really presented the next world as much more than a continuation of this one and the people in it as very little different in the fundamentals to how they were here.

Now, this may be the experience of a certain section of humanity. They may find themselves in an environment that reflects what they are within, and if they are not particularly spiritually attuned in this life, nor will they be in the next. But death in the real spiritual sense must mean something more than just relinquishing the physical body. To take away its deep existential significance, as spiritualism tends to do, is to diminish something that should be of profound relevance to the near trite. If death is tamed and made almost comfortable it will not be the transformative experience it should be. The true heavenly world must be unimaginable in terms of this world, even if it contains all that is good in this world.

Modern man has lost sight of the beauty of death. Isn't that a strange word to choose to describe something so often seen as full of terror and horror, something that signifies loss and suffering? Perhaps it is and I am certainly not recommending a "half in love with easeful death" attitude. To seek or wish for death is a spiritual sin because it is an evasion of responsibility. But the beauty of death lies in its transformative power and reward for a job well done. When your work here is over and you have been true to your calling as an incarnated soul, then death comes as a release from the trivial mundanities of mortal existence and the entry into a higher state of being. The only people who need fear death (as in be frightened of, we should all have an attitude of humble awe before it as we should before any profound mystery) are those, unfortunately numerous now, who deny life because life is far more than worldly, material things, and death, rightly considered, is the doorway to greater life.

Death is the end of term, perhaps a slightly superficial way of looking at it in view of what I have just written but nonetheless one that indicates its aspect of release from labour. But what are the holidays like, whether these be permanent as in the one life only scenario or temporary according to the reincarnation pattern? The general idea is that the sort of afterlife we experience is dependent on how we have acquitted ourselves during this life and also what we believe, truly believe in the heart not just intellectually. If you believe in God and still lie, cheat and all the rest, you clearly don't really believe in God.

So, what we have done and what we believe leave their effect on the mind, which is the only thing we take with us after death. Because the afterlife is a realm of mind, what we experience, our outer, reflects what we are or think, our inner. Therefore, if we have rejected God in mortal life our consciousness reflects that, it is a God-rejecting sort of consciousness, and our post-mortal existence will as well. Similarly, the depth of quality of God we have responded to in life will determine the depth of quality of our spiritual experience in the afterlife.

One of the most encouraging things my teachers said to me was that they **looked forward to being reunited with me.** They also spoke of the **heavenly plane which was my home** and of **the love, beauty and music of the higher worlds where, after fulfilling my duty in this world, I would one day return.** No details, that was not how they worked, and I was a young man at the time who needed to get his feet firmly fixed on the ground and not fly away into dreams. But there was encouragement and just enough indication of the reality of the life after death, which was depicted not just as a better continuation of this world but as something qualitatively different with added dimensions of being. I would imagine that this is something all those who strive to live life according to God's will, notwithstanding the many times when one falls short, can hope for.

Whether it is the real heaven, though, is a different matter. When Christ said that "in my Father's house, there are many mansions (or rooms)", he might have been referring to the idea that there are many planes of existence. We can envisage the physical plane as one of the lowest, probably the lowest as far as human beings are concerned, where matter is furthest removed from spirit or substance is most condensed, and then imagine various higher planes which go right up to the throne of God. I am not going to speculate on how these might proceed. For those who are interested, esoteric literature presents a number of conceptual frameworks, most of which are based on phenomenal planes relating to lower levels of being, emotional and mental worlds, going through spiritual and on to divine worlds. This makes sense as far as it goes but perhaps we shouldn't take it too literally. However, according to this way of looking at the picture, the soul or higher self which sends down an aspect of itself to the physical world for experience and expression would be situated above the phenomenal worlds but below the divine, and the latter would be where the resurrected soul would make its entry into the Kingdom of Heaven. The spiritual level would be where the soul originates, either in a reincarnation scenario or from the point of view of pre-mortal existence. It has to go down in order to eventually go up. Death would see the incarnated self seek to work its way back upwards to the soul level though how far and how fast, and maybe if at all, depends entirely on the quality of life lived and state of consciousness.

This raises the point, what happens to the soul if its earthly self has rejected God? The soul on its own level does not have the opportunity to make a choice. It is in a spiritual world and the question does not arise. But in a material world where the inner and the outer have been completely separated, it does and this is one of the purposes of such a world. It tests the mettle of the soul. The incarnated soul has to make a choice and it has to do this in an environment in which a real choice is possible. Here on Earth there can be no definitive proof of God and this is one of the great virtues of the present time. Previously, when humanity was less intellectually developed and therefore less able to make a free and independent choice, almost everyone believed. Now, belief is totally free, not just because it is not enforced externally but also because we are sufficiently developed to make a decision, no longer spiritual babies.

As we have seen, the soul may be defined as our spiritual self, but this is in relation to the earthly, phenomenal self with which we are familiar in this material world. The soul is not perfect or, at least, not brought to full perfection. It lacks full agency, and this is why it needs to experience life in the physical world, a world that is perceived as separate from God. If the soul, through its earthly persona, turns to God at a time when it knows separation from God, that demonstrates that its inner compass is true. It has the choice it does not have on its own level and it has chosen well. Its choice is in harmony with life. But if the soul, again through its earthly persona, does not turn to God, this demonstrates it has chosen evil (evil being defined as non-God) as opposed to good. Its inner orientation has been shown to be false, basically pointing to itself as prior rather than to God and this is always possible because of the nature of freedom. This cannot be demonstrated on its own level where the reality of divine being is evident. It is only when the soul descends to a world of good and evil that its essential nature can be brought out through revealing how it reacts to the choice of God or no God. Both possibilities are given to it in this world. The fact of God should be clear to the unclouded mind, but we are given grounds for plausible denial. If you don't want to believe, you don't have to.

The soul may be spiritual, but it is not, in Christian parlance, resurrected. We have made the distinction between spiritual and divine, with the one conceived merely as non-material while the other is fully and consciously aligned with God. If the soul through its worldly self choses God then that soul is saved and will eventually, when fully purified of all residual sin, be resurrected. It will ascend to heaven. It is not currently in heaven but in a spiritual zone between earth and heaven. This is a zone of peace and happiness but one in which God is felt rather than known. There is bliss and love, but these are largely passive in contradistinction to the creative freedom and active love of the heavenly world. In terms of luminescence, you might envisage it as a place of moonlight rather than radiant sunlight.

On the other hand, if the soul, through its earthly self, rejects God then that soul will, in terms of spiritual consciousness, fall instead of rise and it will find itself in a world that reflects its internal state. Hell, as an environment, is the reflection of the inner consciousness of the individual soul who goes there. A darkened mind will find itself in a corresponding locale.

To ascend to heaven the soul needs to fill itself with light.

This light must come from Christ. Within each soul there is an image of Christ but this image can only become spiritually vivified when, like a candle lit by a flame, it is lit by Christ himself and that can only happen when the soul in this world opens itself up to Christ. This must be the true Christ not some mind-created earthly facsimile of him, and that means that the individual human mind must be responding to the true soul image which it can only do by going beyond its earthly mind to the spiritual imagination. If it fails to do this that is another form of death, spiritual death, but this, unlike the physical sort, is something over which we have full control. Do not fear physical death. Fear rather the death of the soul which is the rejection of God.

* * *

Mentioning the fear of physical death raises an issue very pertinent for the times in which we live. I am writing this during the coronavirus scare. One of the reasons we have reacted to this scare with what seems like near panic, to the point that it has overwhelmed all other considerations such as the economy, children's education and loss of liberty, is that we no longer believe in God. Our physical safety and security become all-important and the threat of death makes us accept almost anything just so we can continue a bit longer. But we will die anyway, and we may as well come to terms with that fact. All lives come to an end and the materialist and atheist will sooner or later have to confront the truth, their truth anyway, that this is it. There is no more. All pleasures have faded and disappeared, past joys and happiness really are past. They are dust and ashes. There is nothing left but pain, suffering and then darkness. Non-existence. There was never any meaning in anything. That's the logical outcome of their beliefs.

This is a truly pitiful state to be in. It leaves the person in it with few options. Some might think there is a kind of bleak heroism in defiance, in saying: I have lived my life and have no regrets. Death, do your worst! Perhaps there is but this is really just bravado. It achieves nothing. And it is prideful. Most people are not able to be like this anyway. They become frightened as so many of us have done in this time of pandemic. The reality of life and death, hitherto perhaps not fully thought about, becomes apparent and they succumb to fear. There is an alternative. It is belief in God and repentance. Some might say it is cowardly to turn to God when you are frightened of death. I would say it is sensible. You can put all your intellectualising aside and just become what you always have been, really, which is a naked child. Become a naked child and turn to God and you will not be left comfortless. Choose light rather than darkness.

Why Are We Born Into The World?

Having looked at death, let's go back to the beginning and consider why we might need to be born into this world and what we have to do while here to learn the lessons of this earthly existence. Do these lessons simply entail learning to see beyond the world and devote ourselves entirely to higher things, in the process becoming completely detached from any sort of earthly focus, or does this mortal life have value and purpose in itself? I believe both these things to be true in their different ways and will try to explain my position here.

Briefly, we have to develop a real individuality before we can go beyond that and reach a conscious I-Thou union with God and so know love in the full spiritual sense. The pronounced duality experienced in this material world enables us first to develop the self and then, if we follow the spiritual path as we should, to transcend the limited identification with it in the union with God.

As someone born in the West, I don't find thinking in Buddhist terms is helpful for me any longer. I appreciate the spiritual wisdom of Buddhism (see the chapter, Buddhism and Christianity) but the Buddhist denial of the self as a valid spiritual entity seems a limited position that does not encompass the full extent of what creation and evolution is all about – effective as it might be from its own perspective. But the advent of Christ and his incarnation as a human being redeemed matter and nature from their fallen state and made it now possible for the whole of Creation to be saved and sanctified rather than, as before, the spiritual need being to escape matter. It is noteworthy that even the Buddhist position changed somewhat after the Incarnation and my contention is that it was the spirit of Christ which was behind such innovations as the idea of the Bodhisattva. The Christ influence spread throughout Eastern religion not by replacing it but by subtly modifying it. Still, that influence is most present where it is most direct.

Thus, our individuality is a real, God-given thing and we have to develop it in a spiritual sense, grow intellect and imagination, ability to act and be creative and so on, but, at the same time, go beyond the limited identification with it into a deeper union with God. But there has to be something to achieve this union. No self means no union. Complete absorption into the All would render the whole spiritual journey pointless as the conclusion would have added nothing to the beginning. Moreover, such an absorption would be the denial of love.

Buddhism confuses the separate self or ego which is a mind-created thing with the real individuality which is a spiritual thing and which, when it has developed sufficiently, can join in a fully conscious union with God. But it must develop to be a fit container for the divine energy, able to express and reflect it.

This means that you don't need to reduce individuality. God wants strong individuals in his kingdom, that's why he created us, but you do need to reduce and then transcend your unique identification with it. Eradicate the ego, yes, which is why humility is the highest Christian virtue, but not the individual. Buddhism cures the sickness by cutting out what it believes to be its root, but Christianity heals the split in the soul, making it whole.

On a personal note, while the above might be regarded as a theoretical presentation, I would cite my experience with discarnate spiritual teachers as demonstrating its practical application and successful achievement. They stood as examples of the individual soul transfigured and raised to spiritual apotheosis. They were fully individual and, at the same time, fully transparent to God.

In this way of looking at spiritual reality, God is a personal God, not just the impersonal absolute. He may have that aspect as well, but it is the aspect of him at rest, asleep you might say.

But in expression, and this whole universe is him in expression, he is a personal God. This is him awake and active or creative. He creates us, human beings, because he is a God of love and because he expresses himself in love. You might say he grows through love. He creates us with free will because love is only real when the beloved is real and the universe is a vastly more interesting place for God if he shares it with other free beings, who may be dependent on him for their being but who have still been granted freedom.

This might sound a little simple, almost childish, but over-philosophising on the question of existence and its purpose takes us away from the essential truth. The Masters always told me that truth was simple and that endlessly thinking about it got one nowhere, but I have to confess that, being a modern person, my tendency sometimes is to theorise when I should allow myself more to feel with the heart. This is not to recommend the abandonment of thought. We have a mind and should use it. But we need to give priority to intuition and then use thought to unpack that, rather than give thought the driver's seat.

God created us because he is a God of love, a God that gives and a God of ceaseless expression who does actually grow through his creation. He creates us as real individuals not mere clones of himself. We are free. But when we are created as pure spiritual beings, we are babies. With vast potential but undeveloped. We are conscious but in a kind of sleep state. If we are to be real, fully self-conscious, spiritual beings then we must unfold that potential. We must, in a way, build ourselves if we are to be ourselves and not just mechanical automata. We can't be created both free and complete.

God gives us the environment in which to do that and it is this material world in which the sense of separation from him is possible. Without that feeling of separation, we could not come to know ourselves. We would remain spiritual babies. But there's a risk. We might come to identify ourselves exclusively with ourselves. Separation might go too far. Any awareness of God at all might be lost. That appears to be what has happened. Whether it is a consequence of the Fall as described in the Book of Genesis or whether it is part of a natural cycle is a matter for debate and I do not want to enter into the ins and outs of that here, other than to say that I am firmly of the belief that there was a derailment of a natural process and that sin and death entered into the equation in a way that might not have been necessary had things gone according to plan. Things went wrong and that is the explanation for much of the state of the world as we see it today. The Incarnation put things back on track, but it is a gift that still needs to be accepted.

So, salvation was not originally a necessary part of the plan and only became so as a result of the Fall. Instead of our evolution, as in spiritual unfoldment, proceeding naturally and almost inevitably, it became something which we had to turn back to and re-embrace. Without the Fall our spiritual development would have proceeded in a smooth, or much smoother, way. We would have experienced duality but not the full and complete separation from God, and therefore been able to develop mind/self without all the negative consequences we now know so well. We would have entered the material world, reaped the benefits to be found there and returned to spirit in full consciousness, having learnt all the lessons of duality. It would have been a journey from unconscious innocence to self-conscious experience and back to innocence again, but now fully conscious and bearing the fruits of experience which are essentially intelligence, agency and love.

The Fall messed up that natural trajectory. We became trapped in material, self-centred consciousness. Matter actually became more material, harder, denser, to the degree that it became impossible for us to get out of it on our own. That is why we needed the incarnation of Christ to re-spiritualise matter and enable us to liberate ourselves from self-identification as material beings. He offered the way for us to get back on track, but we have to accept that.

This means there are two things going on here. There is the natural spiritual unfoldment that requires spiritual infants to experience this material world in order to fully awaken to themselves and then consciously return to God. That was the original plan. But then there was the corruption of the Fall which locked those infants in separation and materialism and stopped the conscious return occurring naturally. The process was stalled halfway with the disastrous results we know and which required the Incarnation. But now we have to reject identification as material beings, the usefulness of that bit is long since done. We have reached the nadir and must turn around and start our journey back to God.

How God Grows

God says in the Old Testament book of Malachi *"I am the Lord. I change not"* while St Paul says in Hebrews 13:8 *"Jesus Christ is the same yesterday, today, and for ever"*. But then we read in Revelation that the One seated on the throne says *"Behold, I make all things new"*. Does that mean he also renews himself and, if so, is there a contradiction?

There is no contradiction. All these statements are true. They just refer to different aspects of divine being.

God never changes. The eternal ground of existence cannot change because it is. It is not something. As God also says of himself *"I am that I am."* The Divine Person is pure, simple, undivided, One without a second. There is no force that can act on him to cause or bring about change. He is the Creator of time and therefore not subject to it. He stands above movement and is not affected by it.

And yet I would maintain that God does indeed grow and he grows through his creation. A clue is given in the passage that follows the statement from Revelation in which God says the following words. *"I am the Alpha and the Omega, the Beginning and the End."* In his being he is above time but in his becoming he works through time and brings about a result in which change, growth, has occurred. The End state is different to, and not just different to but more than, better than, the Beginning state.

To say that God grows implies he wants to grow but how can God have desires? Wouldn't that make him not God, something that is not whole and lacks completion? How can what is absolute and illimitable grow? Taken literally, that might not make sense. On the level of the absolute there can be no growth because there is no relativity, no becoming, so the idea of more is meaningless. However, we must be careful not to let our imagination be restricted by human concepts. God is not bound by our idea of the absolute any more than he is by our idea of the relative. These are human categories not divine ones. We can reasonably assume that he comes into manifest existence through creation in order to experience himself and his potentials more fully. Having done that, having come into being in the dualistic world of form, he seeks expansion within that world. He seeks to become ever more, which is now possible as a result of the creative tension between the two poles of existence, spirit and matter, subject and object, required for creation to take place. God does not need to do this because of some lack or incompleteness in himself but his creative power to express himself is part of his total reality. If he could not do this, he would be deficient in something, which would be a limitation. Thus, while God as absolute being cannot grow, there is not just this side to him and through his self-expression he can grow. It's not a question of something imperfect seeking perfection but of the already complete and perfect constantly transcending itself and becoming more. Darkness is darkness and that's it but light can become ever brighter. There may be a physical limitation, I don't know, but there is no spiritual one.

Some spiritual systems see God the impersonal absolute and God the Creator as being on different rungs of the metaphysical ladder, with the latter on a lower level of reality. I think this again is forcing human conceptual limitations onto the divine and reflects an intellectual approach rather than a truly spiritual one. If you are thinking in terms of these categories they are better conceived of as God in passive and active modes, sleeping and waking, you might say. But really the essence of divine reality is not in unexpressed beyond being. It is in the fact of I AM. God is certainly beyond form as we might conceive it and cannot be regarded as a separate being out there or as an object of consciousness that we can know and encounter. How could that which created form be bound by it? Nevertheless, God has Individuality. His is the fundamental or primal 'I AM' that is reflected in us as our own sense of individuality. That is what being made in his image means. It is also his individuality that is expressed in creation and the particular form it takes, which is why contemplating the created world can give us a clue as to the nature of God so long as we bear in mind that the world, as we experience it, is not in a state of grace at the moment. The fact that God is personal can be known through feeling his presence and his love. And he grows through this love as it radiates out through created beings who expand the whole of life as they grow individually. God is both immanent and transcendent, within and beyond his creation. He grows through the aspect of immanence.

This truth that God seeks to develop himself through his creation is why those who attempt to see themselves as pure being or pure consciousness are missing out on something important. God gave us a self for us to grow and expand its consciousness. To be sure, this does eventually require uniting it to something greater than itself as in **forget the personal self and merge with the universal self.** We do eventually get to the point at which the only way to continue to grow spiritually is to give up the limited self, as Jesus demonstrated for us on the cross. But that does not mean the gift of self was a mistake or that self is an illusion. It is the sense of separateness, resulting from identification with form, that is the mistake. The self must be given up as a self-sacrifice in love and then it will find a greater identity in God but in that union the individual self, purified, transformed and sanctified, remains. We are not intended to kill or deny the self but to accept its redemption in and through Christ.

* * *

God is always and forever complete and perfect, and nothing can be added to or taken away from him. But through involvement in time and through creating self-conscious beings with freedom and individuality, he increases. This is something that can only happen in a world of change and becoming, so you might say that the reason for this whole world of creation, including, and especially, us, is so that God may grow through self-expression. The religions which tend to emphasise the Absolute and pure being and consequently downgrade the personal God such as, in their different ways, Buddhism and Advaita Vedanta, don't properly appreciate the relevance of creation and so have only half the truth. For God is not the impersonal absolute but dynamic, creative, individual being.

You can reconcile the fact of the perfection of God with the idea that he changes and grows by saying that changelessness is a kind of limitation. And if God is infinite and unlimited then surely he cannot be restricted to changelessness? He must include the possibility of change, too, and so he creates to become more; always complete but always moving on to greater levels of completion. You can quibble and say this only relates to him as he is in expression or in his active mode but creativity is an essential and fundamental part of the divine nature. Without it, being would be static.

I first came to this way of thinking because I had to work out why I had an intuitive rejection of the Buddhist and rigid non-dualist points of view and disagreed with all those who believed that reality was impersonal, with the personal just an illusion to be transcended by the wise. For it seemed to me that the personal is the whole point of why there is something rather than nothing, and that God fully and equally encompasses both what the earthly mind would describe as absolute and relative, and there is no contradiction in that inclusive approach. Rather the contradiction lies in asserting that a purely impersonal reality could ever give rise to the personal. And if the impersonal is deemed to be the sole ground of reality, with the personal somehow (how?) arising from that, then to say that God is love is a meaningless statement instead of the fundamental truth which we know it to be. It's not enough to say that this statement is true in the relative world. If it's not true right down to the bedrock of existence, then it's not true in any meaningful way at all.

Christ came to redeem fallen nature. Through his incarnation the broken bridge between the spiritual and material worlds was re-established, and not just for mankind but for the whole of creation. The Father grows through the activity of the Son, who by his birth as a man made it possible for the material world, hitherto cut off from spirit, to be reconnected to its source. The infusion of spirit into matter through Christ began the reconsecration of the earth, disrupted at the Fall, and allowed for the eventual spiritualisation of matter and its translation into heaven, both for individual souls and for the whole of the creation. God could once again begin to grow in the way intended, and we with him.

The Spiritualisation of Matter

We naturally tend to think of religion and spirituality from our own point of view, but how might it be regarded from God's perspective? Does he actually gain anything when a soul consciously turns to him and contributes its being to the kingdom of heaven? From the angle of the absolute, clearly not. Infinity plus one still equals infinity. But I believe this is the wrong way to look at it. Every soul that undergoes the process of theosis or divinisation increases God's knowledge of himself. He becomes more. Love grows, consciousness expands. The totality of divine life is enriched. I might be accused of applying finite measures to the infinite, but I think that this is the point of creation, to become more. God is not just the unbounded absolute (whatever that means, it's really just an intellectual abstraction that covers up our ignorance of what lies beyond the phenomenal world), he is the Father of Heaven and Earth, intimately connected to each and every part of his creation, especially the human part which represents him inside the created world.

Unless we understand that God had a purpose in creation and have some inkling of what that purpose might be, we will find it hard to play our part, and, believe it or not, we all do have a part to play. We are all actors in a grand cosmic drama, but this drama is not just for fun or entertainment. It is creative and it has a goal. We are each entrusted with an individual self, a real spiritual entity that is wholly ours, and our task is to nurture and develop that self and then add its 'weight' as a contribution to the whole, thus magnifying creation.

The universe is the product of two complementary forces, the two poles of being, which are spirit and matter, otherwise conceived of as subject and object, inner and outer, even light and darkness. It is the interaction between these two forces which produces growth and development. But they are not equal. That is a misapprehension based on applying material considerations, ones relating to quantitative measurement, to spiritual realities. However, they are not unequal either. That again comes from framing the question incorrectly. They are complementary and different, and yet the material should always be seen in the light of the spiritual rather than the other way around. This is very important and the failure to understand this has produced all sorts of what must be considered spiritual perversions, ranging from materialism to leftist utopianism and even humanism. There is also the opposite error of considering spirit as something that renders matter immaterial, if I can use that word. This is the error of those who would deny the self instead of presenting it, purified and humble, as a gift to God to use for the expansion of his creative project.

I make this point because a number of Westerners attracted to Eastern forms of mysticism in the spiritual desert of the 21st century become rather like materialists in that they deny part of reality. In the case of the materialist, what is denied is spirit. In the case of what are known as non-dualists, who follow various forms of Buddhism or Hindu Vedanta, what is denied is matter or, at least, its authentic nature and creative purpose. The wise spiritual aspirant seeks to bring matter into harmony with spirit and so does not deny his individual self but submits it to spiritual discipline by various means including prayer and contemplation, cultivating love of the good and whatever form of service and sacrifice he may be called to. If all goes well this leads eventually to the union of the soul with God. The theoretical non-dualist, on the other hand, dismisses the individual self as illusion, rejecting it as something ultimately non-existent. But he is throwing away the very thing that will fulfil his true purpose. At best, he will find himself re-absorbed into the pool of universal consciousness from which God drew souls. He will know bliss and peace, but he will not know God and nor will he have gone beyond creation, albeit in its inner aspects, to the true heaven of resurrected souls who have entered into communion with the Creator. That's at best. It is actually more likely he will just lock himself into a mind-created non-dualistic thought form, where he will remain until the hard knocks of life bring him to his senses.

The true task for each human soul is to bring the material side of its nature under the dominance of the spiritual. Human beings are unique, as far as we know, in that they do have material and spiritual sides. They, in their person, combine the two poles of the universe in a way that nothing else does. Angels are spiritual, animals are material. But human beings are both, and the human soul is where the two forces meet. Our work lies in rising up matter (in us) to the point at which it may be overshadowed by spirit, thus transforming the whole into a new creation. Spirit and matter having been sundered from their original unity before creation are re-united consciously. This cannot be done if matter is rejected. It needs the union of spiritual and material to make a real spiritual self, a new being of light which can swell the numbers and the glory and the brilliance of the Heavenly Host.

Duality is a fundamental principle of the universe and exists for a reason. Everything comes from the interplay between the two poles which are two and, at the same time, one. We need to transcend our current identification with outer form or matter, that is quite true. We need to see duality as the expression of the one reality of God, that is also true. But we do this through fully integrating the two poles of existence within our individual being, not by denying the creative potency of one of them. Non-dualists are not wrong to regard the Father as root reality but the Father can only be known by the Son, who is born from the union of Father and Mother, otherwise, spirit and matter, in the secret place of the heart.

God's purpose in creation is the spiritualisation of matter, which is the conversion of darkness into light and is the real task required of the disciple. You do not make base metal into gold by throwing away the base metal but by purifying and refining it to the point at which real transmutation can take place. Likewise, you do not awaken spiritually by denying your soul but by cleansing it, perfecting it and then, only when all that has been achieved, offering it up in sacrifice, at which point it will be transformed.

When Jesus ascended into heaven, he took his body with him. This is a most profound truth and foreshadows what is intended to happen to the entire Earth at the end of the age. The whole of life, once cleansed of those parts that will not fully open themselves to the divine word and accept the pattern of Christ, will be raised up into spirit, the unity of which will be enriched by a glorious multiplicity. The purpose of creation, which is to bring about love and beauty and conscious knowledge of the good, will be fulfilled.

The World Was Damaged but Has Been Healed

In the opening chapter of this book I claimed that this world was perfect for its intended purpose which was as an environment in which the soul might grow through experience and expression. However, I appreciate some readers may still find the idea of the world as a school, with the educational aim of providing a locale for trial, difficulty and suffering, insufficient to account for its actual state. Even with that excuse, does the world have to be quite as bad as it sometimes is? Need suffering be as severe as it can turn out to be? Something else appears to be going on. What might that be?

A materialist would say there is no need to look for an explanation. The world is as it is because there is no meaning, no purpose to it and therefore we can expect what we see, which is a mixture of what to us seems good and bad, but really there is no good and bad unless we make it so. But this is a superficial explanation which disregards vast chunks of our experience and ignores intuition, not to mention revelation and the spiritual insights of millions of people. It might provide some kind of rationale for evil and suffering as we experience them but at the expense of dismissing so much else that is just as significant in our lives, from love, to the sense of beauty, to the yearning for truth and so on.

So, where else can we look for an understanding of the prevalence of suffering in the world?

Perhaps, first of all, we should look to the teaching of the Fall in which human disobedience to spiritual truth was the initial cause of suffering and death. In some sense, we turned away from the good and decided to place ourselves at the centre of life instead of God. By rejecting God, which we did if he was no longer central, we created an environment in which suffering and death became possible.

But I don't think even that is sufficient explanation. It does explain much of what we experience, but not everything. Not the depth of evil in the world. To get a fuller picture, I believe we have to accept that there are spiritual forces that seek our ill. These forces work against God and they have sufficient power to damage God's plan for humanity, in the short term anyway. Now, God could eradicate these forces in an instant if he chose, but that would probably mean bringing his experiment with humanity to an end because this experiment requires the existence and exercise of free will.

These dark forces do have power, but it is a limited sort of power and they cannot affect us on an individual level unless we allow them into our spiritual orbit through manifesting negative energy, otherwise known as sin, ourselves. The Masters frequently warned me about attack from evil forces but said that if I did not react to them in thought they would go away. They have no power if one does not allow oneself to descend to their level. As for who or what they might be, they are the fallen angels and those human souls that have allowed themselves to be corrupted by them. They are combatted by God's angels on a spiritual level, meaning the non-material realms between the heavenly planes (to which they cannot gain access due to the darkness in their being, like attracting like on these levels) and the physical world. But we must also counter their attacks in our hearts and minds.

All spiritual teachings worthy of the name recognise that this world is a battleground between good and evil. The dark forces have damaged the world and made of it a worse place than it might have been but God allows their existence because the purpose of creation is spiritual freedom and he has renounced some of his power to allow for that. If he overrode our freedom, he would effectively have to destroy the world. The myth of the Flood tells us that he has done precisely that in the past.

It might be asked why God didn't foresee the Fall and the events that led to the Flood and do something to prevent these. Again, the answer is free will, but we must also say that God does not see the future before it happens. For him, the future is now. God does not experience time as we do. He does experience it, but he sees all time as now. Past, present and future are all now to him. So, there is no conflict between free will and the fact that God knows the future. He does not know it before it happens because to him it is happening in some eternal present. Thus, he sees it but does not determine it.

The world may have been damaged but this cannot deflect God's ultimate purpose. It did, however, require a change of plan, a dramatic intervention which was the most important thing ever to have happened in this world. I refer of course to the birth of Christ. Christ's birth, life, death and resurrection healed the world of the harm done by the Fall and defeated Satan. Satan still has power but only what we allow him if we reject the life of the spirit. Henceforth, anyone can banish him and his works simply by turning to Christ and inviting him into their heart. It really is as simple as that. But it must be the true Christ we invite and not some manufactured image that imitates him. For sometimes we project our idea of Christ, a Christ who fits in with our prejudices and preconceptions, onto the real Christ and then take the imitated projection for the reality. We can have a 'gentle Jesus, meek and mild' or a Jesus who teaches love but not truth (or vice versa) or a Jesus who turns a blind eye to sin in the name of acceptance of everyone or a Jesus who offers forgiveness regardless of repentance or a Jesus preaching justice without mercy (or vice versa) and many other sorts of fake Jesus based on our own ignorance and desires. None of these will help us. They are all false idols.

We can only know the real Christ if we reject the world and follow his commandments, the chief of which is to love God, and therefore truth, above all else. If there is anything that comes before this, then we are not following Jesus but ourselves in some way. To avail ourselves of the healing offered by Christ we have to take the medicine and that does not always taste pleasant to the earthly self. It's rather like the rich young man who thought he had done everything required but when it finally came to the point, he could not cross the threshold between acceptance and denial.

I am not saying no one can lead a proper spiritual life if they are not Christian but I think that paths without Christ are incomplete. C. S Lewis's insight in *The Last Battle* regarding Emeth the Calormene who followed Aslan in his heart without knowing him outwardly strikes me as pertinent here. If we follow the light of Christ as it shines within our own heart, we are closer to him than if we follow him outwardly alone. No doubt, in this case, there will remain work to be done after departing this world but then that is true for all of us except the greatest saints. And no doubt, too, it is easier to follow Christ in our hearts when we follow him outwardly, too, but we have to accept that God has provided different paths at different times and some of them may actually include important elements of truth neglected in established Christianity.

But I am going off the point, which is that despite the damage inflicted on the world by the fallen angels in the past and at the present time, God remains in charge. That is hard to believe sometimes but only because we can't see the whole picture. If we could then the hardships we endure now would not seem so bad. The world has been healed by the entry into it of Jesus and from now on, however dark it may seem, we should know that a bright future is promised for those who accept the gift that Christ offers. This world is still a school and work, hard work, still needs to be done to pass our examinations. It is also true that there are higher and lower grades of success, ranging from the saints to ordinary believers. But when we take Christ for our teacher, success is guaranteed.

A Reflection of the Present Time

We have just spoken of the damage inflicted by the fallen angels. To anyone whose spiritual eyes are open there is something deeply unusual about the times in which we live. These are no ordinary times. The almost universal spiritual apostasy would indicate that, if nothing else did, but there are, in fact, plenty of other signs that we are currently living through a period that approximates to the Biblical end times. These are the times when spiritual goodness and truth are chased from the world, evil forces run riot and values are inverted, with hierarchical distinctions levelled off or turned on their head. Matter becomes dominant and spirit is forgotten and denied. This is a process that has been gathering pace for more than a century (see the Cycles of Change chapter) but it has really been stepped up since the turn of the millennium and has taken a new and more serious turn in 2020, when I write these words.

At the end of an age, matter actually becomes denser so that the spiritual world is increasingly obscured. Can you not feel that the quality of consciousness is becoming more self-enclosed? If you could weigh it, it would be heavier. If you could see it, it would be darker. This is a metaphysical reality, though not measurable by scientific instruments made of the same matter that is condensing. How should we react to this? By accepting it as real and going along with life as it now appears to be? Or by holding fast to the truth within, to our inner knowledge of the reality of God, which may be obscured but is not obliterated by this thickening of the psychic atmosphere?

Clearly, the latter. This is the test of the present time. Who succumbs to the darkness and who resists it. The world is once more killing God as it did 2,000 years ago but this time when he rises again it will be in the hearts of those that have left a place for him.

Meanwhile the spiritual darkness will increase. That is an inevitable part of the process of an age coming to its end. The end of not just a term or a year but of school, with final exams taken and grades awarded. The quality of human civilisations will continue to decline. Evil, spiritual evil, will spread with even potentially progressive movements infiltrated and subverted to work against their original impulse. But, unpleasant as this is to live through, we are still privileged to be born at a time when God is giving those who hear his voice a great opportunity to make strides forward in their spiritual growth. All we really have to do is hold fast to the truth within amidst the lies of the world. It is a great testing of the human heart. No longer can we rely on anything external, but this has the effect of forcing us to throw away our crutches and rely on ourselves. We are being pushed into spiritual independence.

In around 1990 my teachers told me that we were currently living during a period of greater vulgarity than at any time in the history of our planet. I believe they knew that history and therefore could speak with authority. What on earth would they say now? Most people of my acquaintance appear to think that things are better than ever today. Only recently I was told that this is the best time to live despite its problems, and this is not just because of greater material ease due to the advantages of a modern technological society. We are kinder, more tolerant, and more equal and this makes us better than our forefathers. I don't doubt we are better in some ways, but the fact is we are a spirit-denying society, and this makes everything about us evil. Yes, I use that word. Not mistaken or in error but evil. Evil is the rejection of God. Certainly, it can have more dramatic manifestations as in violence and cruelty but those are just particular sorts of evil. The heart that is closed to God lives as a material being, even if it has some spiritual goals, and this makes it open to all kinds of spiritual, as opposed to material, evil. The behaviour of a material being does get increasingly vulgar (to use the Master's word) because, losing touch with higher reality and truer values, it becomes debased, focused on its material self and the goals and pleasures of that self. Material pleasure is not wrong but it should never be seen as primary, let alone all there is. It must always be known in the light of our reality as spiritual beings.

Once you abandon God, you abandon reality. That is what we have done. It explains why the natural way is rejected now and anything that happens to exist in any form is regarded as equally valid as anything else that happens to exist. When the spiritual order, the vertical hierarchy of being, is denied, the horizontal or natural order cannot stand since it has its roots in the spiritual. Now, we have no roots. We are blown about in any direction dictated by the worldly powers because there is nothing else against which we can measure truth. Past generations may have lost their spiritual understanding, but they still had the worldview built by that understanding and it was the determining part of their experience of what life was. But this worldview has been chipped away at and gradually demolished over the past few decades and the speed of demolition has increased dramatically since the turn of the millennium, coincidentally or not. I actually feel the solar eclipse in August 1999 marked a definite shift from a time when the old world still had some authoritative power to one in which new ways became completely in the ascendant. They are now the norm.

The only thing we have that is wholly our own is our will, our capacity to make a free choice. This is the part of us that is actually independent of God. That is why what we decide to believe is of critical importance. From the acceptance or rejection of God comes everything else. Clearly, it must be a proper acceptance. It must be God we accept not some kind of projected image we might make of him, and it must be an acceptance of the heart not just the mind, as appears to be the case with so many of the current church leaders whose understanding of God is filtered through a basically secular worldview. The present time is the result of a mass turning away of the human will that now seeks its own independent fulfilment, rather than fulfilment in God which is the only true fulfilment. The modern world may have been inspired by forces of spiritual evil, but it has been chosen by us. We cannot claim innocence. We may have been manipulated and deceived but nothing obliged us to succumb to that. It was a free choice on our part, and we will have to live with the consequences of that choice.

Today we are faced with a false good and a true good. The false good is the apparent good of this world. It is presented as political good, humanitarian good, social good, the Utopian good of an ideal society. Basically, any good without God. It is the good of the human race considered primarily as human beings and without reference, or with just token reference, to their Creator who is also their properly destined end. It is not just a question of a different kind of good but of a counterfeit good which is actually evil because it redirects spiritual qualities such as love and intelligence into material channels seeking earthly benefit. But it is even worse than that. It is not just spiritually neutral but anti-spiritual. The 20th century was largely spiritually neutral, for the majority of ordinary people anyway. The 21st has become anti-spiritual because even the forces that pretend to good in the material realm are often motivated by hatred and the desire for destruction. I do not think we can escape this, and even to try to stand against it outwardly, thinking that the tide can somehow be turned, is a mistake. It is part of an inevitable entropic process. We should always proclaim our opposition to it but not in the hope that this will have any effect other than for those relatively few individuals who look for light in a world of increasing darkness. These are the end times, when our hope must be in God and he never fails those who place their hope in him.

But what about those who don't? The strange thing about the present times is that they are both extraordinary and just plain dull. Nothing of any real interest is taking place even though the events of 2020 were both dramatic and unprecedented. But none of it really means anything as nothing can mean anything in the absence of God. Now he has been forgotten for so long that in most people's minds he has become like Odin or Zeus, merely an old tribal god we have long since outgrown. Unfortunately, this simply means that human beings have begun to lose the will to live, though they are still afraid of death. Without a spiritual background to life, it becomes merely a sorry succession of moments of seeking pleasure which eventually palls and then all that matters is avoiding pain. Our science is no longer the search for truth and understanding about the universe but a kind of technocratic support system for a particular ideology. Our art is the product of mediocre minds digging into the body of the past and thinking they are making something new by chopping up the corpse. And our religion, what there is of it, amounts to little more than warming up the leftovers of a feast, most of which has long since been eaten so the nourishment is meagre.

But I am neither a pessimist nor a cynic. I believe that God is always there and will reward those who remain faithful to the vision of holiness. The world in its present form is unlikely to survive but that is not a bad thing. Corruption needs to be cleansed. But souls will survive in one form or another and they will go to where their mind takes them. In the spiritual world we get what we are. In the meantime, this world will become increasingly mad. What is there to love or honour or aspire to? Just an abstraction called humanity but humanity on its own is not much. With God we are the most extraordinary and glorious beings. Without him we are just a lot of clever but foolish monkeys, chattering about nothing but full of self-importance.

In 1924, at a lecture in Holland, the spiritual philosopher, or spiritual scientist as he thought of himself, Rudolf Steiner said that by the year 2000 *"humanity will either stand at the grave of all civilisation or at the beginning of that age when in the souls of human beings who unite intelligence with spirituality in their hearts the Archangel Michael's battle will be fought out to victory."* It's not hard to see which of those two options is the one that happened. Pretty much everything that could go wrong in the 20th century, especially the latter half, did go wrong. The Nazis and the Communists were defeated on the physical plane, but the battle carried on at spiritual levels and we proved too weak and too inept to wage it successfully. We succumbed to the anti-spiritual forces that had been let loose. The higher impulses that had played on human consciousness were reacted to, but they were reacted to on the material plane and misinterpreted as relating to earthly man instead of his spiritual self. This is why so-called progressive movements believe themselves to be at the vanguard of humanity. They have responded to the real progressive impulses but they have done so in a regressive manner, from the lower self, and they have corrupted and debased that which should have carried us forward into a new age of spiritual understanding.

The dreams of those who thought we would be entering the Age of Aquarius in the new millennium have turned out to be false, in no small part because many of the proponents of this idea thought they could be spiritual without being Christian, perhaps because this does not demand the full recognition that one is a sinner in need of redemption. While there may be a Golden Age in the future, I rather doubt humanity in its present form will be here to see it. We really are not worthy. Repentance is always possible but the last twenty years has shown that to be extremely unlikely, certainly in the mass – individuals are a different matter. Steiner's thought that *"in the souls of human beings who unite intelligence with spirituality in their hearts the Archangel Michael's battle will be fought out to victory"* still applies on an individual level. So, for those of us who recognise the signs of the times, all we need do now, all we can do now, is watch and pray in the sure knowledge that God is there even in this most testing of times.

The Test of Today

As the pace of change quickens it will become ever clearer that now really is the time of a great testing of human beings. That is the only explanation for the state of the world today and why so much falsehood is presented as truth in the public forum and then allowed such a free rein. We are being weighed in the balance, subjected to tests of heart and mind to find if we are worthy of entering into a state of spiritual truth. In order to achieve this, we often have to go against the flow of apparent right thinking instead of with it as might have been the case in earlier times. That is because only if we do this can it really be known that we are heeding the truth from inside ourselves, hence properly responding to God and not just following the path as it might have been imposed on us from outside. We now often have to follow the line of *most resistance*. So, we have to show both faith and courage, insight and the strength of mind to bear witness to it.

One of the tests of the contemporary world is to see if we accept a lesser good as absolute and thereby reject the greater one. The lesser good is the well-being of humanity considered as separate from God. This goes some way towards explaining the success of liberal doctrines and how they have become identified with goodness and virtue. These doctrines might have had some validity if this world were all that life had to offer but since that is absolutely not the case, they fall far short of what is needed. They are predicated on the basis that there is no Creator with a purpose that goes beyond our immediate happiness and fulfilment in this world, and that, insofar as a human being is concerned, what you see is all there is. They rely for their truth on a denial of God (which makes it strange that so many religious people, especially those in roles of authority, adopt them), and they emphasise the second of

Christ's commandments (love your neighbour) at the expense of the first (love God). Of course, even love of one's neighbour is only observed theoretically and as a means of signalling that you are on the right side. Incidentally, I find that loving your distant neighbour is now used as an excuse to pay less attention to your near one, demonstrating that love has little to do with it and is just used as an excuse to dismantle traditional structures of truth and rob them of their spiritually protective qualities.

Be that as it may, the fact is that the second commandment can only be truly observed when the first is achieved. That is because all love flows from God. He is the source of love and if you try to love while denying the source, you are attempting the impossible. You cannot love in a spiritual sense, which means truly love, unless you are at least somewhat aware of the reality of God. There is no love without God. You can be aware of the idea or fact of love because God is within you whether you acknowledge him or not, but this idea can only really come into being when you open your heart and mind up to God or Christ, who is his human face and form. If you can't do this, then what you call love will be like a copy of something rather than the thing itself. It will never catch fire until it is touched by the flame of God. One might concede that liberal doctrines have some truth in them but if so, it is the truth of a counterfeit rather than that of the genuine article. Indeed, liberalism might be considered just that, a counterfeit of Christianity. A Christianity flattened out, robbed of transcendence, materialised, secularised and brought down to this world. An imposter and pretender. It was probably specifically designed to replace the real thing by apparently retaining the good bits but throwing out the superstitions. In fact, it does the precise opposite and keeps the shell while discarding the nut. But then those who oppose liberal doctrines must take care that they do not fall into the extreme of denying these have any validity at all, even on a relative level. If you oppose the follies of modern forms of liberalism, you must not let that push you into the opposite extreme. Remember there are two commandments, love God and love your neighbour as yourself. The latter must be seen in the light of the former but if you neglect the latter then you become almost as bad as those who neglect or deny God. This, too, is part of the test of today. Don't let the lies of the enemy lead you into the over-reaction of rejecting the reality of the truth he presents in a corrupted and materialised state.

Many previous generations have felt they were living during the end times as predicted in the New Testament. This has always been a fallen world. But today there seems little doubt, not just because Christianity is less and less followed in lands where it has held sway for centuries, but also because what calls itself Christianity now is no longer the real thing, having increasingly become quite another set of beliefs that have simply assumed the Christian name and outer form. Wherever the transcendent Creator takes second place to the needs, wishes and requirements of earthly man and has to fit into those, you can be sure that what you are seeing is not the religion of Christ, whose kingdom is not of this world.

The increasing polarisation of the last few years has made it seem that we are coming closer to a fork in the road, where a real choice has to be made in that two alternatives will be available to us and we can no longer hedge our bets. We will have to decide whether to serve God or Man, though, naturally, the choice will not be presented in so unsubtle a form as that. In fact, some people might think they are serving God when they are not at all. This is something we must all watch out for. Jesus's words in Matthew 7:21 might apply to any one of us if we are not careful. *"Not everyone who says to Me, 'Lord, Lord,' shall enter the kingdom of heaven, but he who does the will of My Father in heaven."*

So, now is the time of spiritual testing. However, my belief is that because God is merciful the majority of those who fall short are not lost but will be consigned to other spheres where their spiritual education will continue in a different school, though this one will be tougher. The physical world is the world of choice and choices made here have consequences which cannot be escaped. God is a God of Mercy, but he is also a God of Justice, and free will is a two-edged sword. We are truly free, which means free to make mistakes. Spiritual refusal has become the norm these days, but it has serious consequences which we would do well to be aware of if we are to avoid these mistakes.

* * *

This raises the interesting question of whether everyone will eventually be saved and enter into the Kingdom of Heaven, understanding that to mean the kingdom of resurrected souls who have evolved out of the created worlds, both material and spiritual, and been found worthy of entering into the presence of the Creator.

It has become almost 'unspiritual' to believe in hell because we think that a God of love could not possibly have made such an environment. The only problem with that idea is that the place where we learn most about a God of love, which is the New Testament, is the same place where there is the most emphasis on hell. Jesus, the incarnation of love, speaks many times and in no uncertain terms about the reality of hell and how those who reject his message may end up there. How can we resolve this apparent contradiction?

Perhaps we can start by saying that God did not create hell. Hell was created by the rejection of God, firstly by fallen angels and then by those humans who joined them in that rejection. A reasonable definition of hell is a place or state where God is not: so how can we blame God for it? We can perhaps blame God for the possibility of it but only because he gave creatures free will to accept or reject him. But we cannot blame him for the fact of it. It exists because it has been created by the created, not by the Creator.

If it does exist, then what is it? Traditional descriptions were undoubtedly intended to convey something of its nature symbolically but they may also be external manifestations of internal states since the idea is that in the afterlife outer and inner become one so our environment is, to a much greater extent than here, a reflection of what is in our mind. Interestingly, this supports the thought that, though hell is undoubtedly a place of spiritual suffering, it may start off in certain cases as a place of material/sensual pleasure, though the law of diminishing returns would apply and the pleasure would soon turn to ashes. This is just speculation but there could well be many different types of hell, corresponding to different types of human vice, as in Dante's depiction of the Inferno. To restrict it to a one size fits all sort of place seems unimaginative.

Be that as it may, the key element of hell is separation. The deepest hell is the state of egotism carried to its ultimate degree where the person is so centred on himself that he is separated from everything else. It is a state where the 'I' has become all there is in the sense that nothing else has any intrinsic reality or value of its own. Everything other than the 'I' is perceived only in terms of its usefulness to that 'I'. And this tells us that not only did God not create hell, he does not send us there either. We send ourselves there by our rejection of him and our refusal to let go of our own separate egos. It may even be that we go there in full knowledge of what we are doing.

But do we stay there? The answer must be that it depends on what we mean by hell. I would say that there are places in the non-physical worlds where souls closed to God go who are not past redemption and for whom there is a way back if they chose to take it. It may be that the great majority of erring souls follow this path. But there is also the possibility of spiritual destruction for if free will means anything it must mean that a definitive choice can be made, from which there is no turning back. It is this spiritual destruction that is the true hell. The lesser or more relative hells are not eternal, in that even here a soul can repent and turn its face to the light. Whether it will or not is entirely down to it, but the possibility is there.

An old problem of thinking of the afterlife in terms of heaven and hell as the only two states possible is how heaven could be heaven if those we love are not there. That is to say, in hell. This is a profound question which we should consider, though obviously without the pretence of offering a definitive solution.

We can start by saying that it is axiomatic that nothing impure can get into heaven. Sinners by definition cannot do so, whether they are those we love or not. But then nor can any of us without God's grace. Therefore, there is always hope, even for the most obdurate of souls. Secondly, we have to ask what is hell? Heaven is surely supreme reality and that implies that hell is actually unreal. How can it be real if it is outside God who is reality itself? Maybe it is only the unreal part of us that goes there. Inside every human being there is something of God and it is that which gives us our reality. This cannot go to hell, so maybe this part of us is always salvaged and made new while the dross is burnt away.

Does this mean that somehow everyone will be saved? That would seem to go against justice and free will. Perhaps in the next world opportunities will exist for every soul to turn round, though the way back will be long and hard for some. But if these opportunities continue to be turned down then it is possible that souls that refuse to blossom as they should are eventually cast into the purifying lake of fire. This fire burns out all individual evil of a created being, in fact all its created part, but the essence of the soul, its divine part which cannot be destroyed, might be preserved to begin again with another chance to grow correctly until this essential part is indeed saved, though the form it takes will not be the same as the one in which it originally appeared. This idea might reconcile the demands of free will, justice and love. We, as individuals, must take the consequences of our actions and beliefs and if we choose not to be resurrected, that is our right. But the part of us which is God himself cannot be destroyed. So, this could come back in a new form until eventually it finds its true being in heaven.

This means Hitler as Hitler may have gone to spiritual destruction but the spiritual essence of Hitler, which cannot be destroyed because it is of God himself, will have a new chance somewhere further down the line in another soul. It is a fresh start and a new person, but it is the same divine reality behind that person. You might say that this is no longer Hitler because he is gone and you would be correct, but the inner truth that anyone may ever have loved in him is still there and would be known, albeit in a quite different form.

These reflections lead me to think that our notions of hell may refer to two different things. The first is a place (or state) of darkened consciousness where those go who have not accepted God in this lifetime but who still have a chance of redemption if they will but receive it. They have created this hell for themselves but there is a way out if they want it and accept what is required to leave. Note that this is different to the idea of purgatory because that is for souls who acknowledge the light but are not yet sufficiently pure to be worthy of it. But the second hell is spiritual destruction of the individual and that is eternal in that it is final. However, it may be that, saved from that destruction, is the divine essence of that soul and this does have a new chance of salvation.

But, as I say, all this is speculation. It is certainly no reason not to seek salvation here and now.

Imagination is Vision

Of all qualities associated with the spiritual path, such as love, virtue, faith and so on, there is one that receives less attention in religious circles but is just as important because it is the faculty that opens up the higher worlds to us and, rightly directed, orients us to these worlds. That quality is imagination.

Many people have felt that a work such as *The Lord of the Rings* seems more real in some way than real life. This is probably something every imaginative reader recognises but few take any further. Specifically, it is not taken to the next logical step, which says it feels more real because it is more real. Not in its details but in its spirit. Why might that be? What is it about myth and fairy tales that gives them their enduring appeal and the sense they have of opening reality up to something greater than normal everyday experience of it allows?

I suggest that good fantasy (that is, fantasy based on imagination rather than fancy, as in Coleridge's important distinction) has at least some of the following elements, and it is the presence of these elements that can make it seem more real than reality. And the reason they can do this is because they are actually true, just not understood as such according to our present limited, semi-mechanistic worldview. We don't know them or accept them with our rational minds but something deep within us responds to them as truth, so that when these ideas are skilfully presented to our imagination, and our imagination is sufficiently finely tuned since it's a two-way process, they have the power to remind us of a time when they were known in the world, which was the time of original participation, when the spiritual world was not fully separate from the material. Alternatively, they can point forward to a future when the essential truth of them is re-acknowledged but in a way that includes our developed mental capacities. As I say, with our outer mind we reject these ideas because from the standpoint of modern science there is no evidence for them, but in our hearts we see that they do indeed correspond to reality – even when we don't believe that in our heads.

A basic part of our contemporary perception of reality is the feeling of separation from the wholeness of life, with a resultant sense of alienation. Imaginative fantasy restores meaning to existence by opening life up to wider horizons or adding dimensions to it that have been lost by our current contracted mode of self-awareness. In order to progress from our earlier passive participation in life to a more pro-active and creative involvement with it our vision had to be narrowed and our sense of reality restricted. We had to lose the feeling of oneness to gain the sense of self. This loss is deeply felt but well written fantasy can give us re-entry into a more inclusive mode of consciousness when it incorporates some or all of the following features. Its purpose is to engage the imagination which, properly understood, is an organ of perception not just an image-making faculty or fabricator of make-believe. It can be that, too, and often is but when functioning correctly and pointing towards the soul it receives impressions from higher worlds, which are not just places but qualities of being and knowing.

Some of the ideas present in myth and fantasy that can make it seem more real than reality are the following. Not all of them are always included but some of them must be.

- Nature is alive as a whole and, in its parts, full of spirits.

- Life extends vertically as well as horizontally so there are aspects of it that we cannot perceive directly now but which can still make an impact in this world.

- Providence is real.

- Good will eventually triumph over evil.

- Such things as beauty and nobility are objective realities and reflections of a higher order of being.

- Archetypes are real things and heroes should correspond to these.

- The outer world of nature reflects the inner world of consciousness and vice versa.

- Feelings of mystery and awe are natural responses to something profound and true.

The list could be continued but the general point is that we currently live in an outer world in which randomness and general purposelessness are the order of the day. Imagination takes us to an inner world of meaning where beauty is truth, and myth and fantasy are bridges into that world insofar as they recognise that there is something behind the scenes of outer appearance.

A final point. None of this means there is anything intrinsically spiritual about myth or fantasy or even imagination, but they can point to the spiritual. The world of myth and fantasy is a middle ground between the material world and the spiritual world, and that is why it seems more real than the former while, in its turn, is less real than the latter.

Will, Imagination and Evil

A common thread running through this book is that we are living in a particularly evil time. In some respects, the worst ever, since evil is essentially the denial of God in whom all good is centred and from whom all good arises. Today, we have moved beyond the spiritual negligence of the 20th century into the active rejection of not only God but his created order as well. Inevitably, when you deny transcendent reality you deny any sort of fixed reality at all because reality is no longer anchored in anything. This is why once God goes, nature and humanity will not be far behind.

People usually point to Hitler as the embodiment of evil in the modern age, but I would maintain that, spiritually speaking, there are people as evil as him living right now who outwardly might appear to be exemplary citizens. If you find this statement shocking let me point out that evil is not just measured by the bad things you do. It is measured by your approach to reality. Reality is God. So, when I use the word evil, I don't simply mean bad in the conventional anti-human sense. I refer to an attitude to life, an attitude towards the Creator. The anti-God sense. An evil attitude sets itself against real goodness and truth which are necessarily spiritual. They must be. If there is no spiritual truth, then nothing has intrinsic reality and good and evil are meaningless terms.

The 20th century had Communism and Nazism which were obvious evils and had to be fought. But in the 21st century the dark powers have changed their tactics and evil takes a softer, subtler form, disguising itself as good, but just as spiritually pernicious, maybe more so as the soul embraces this spiritual evil willingly in the belief that it is being virtuous. This would not happen if the soul were rightly ordered and less fixated on itself and its material nature to the detriment of God and its higher being in him. But it does happen because the soul gives itself to a false good, a good based on its own fallen desires and beliefs.

The false good is the religion of humanity in which natural and spiritual differences are denied, the higher brought down to the level of the lower and the fact of spiritual evil as a real thing dismissed as a prejudice of the ignorant, to believe in which is actually hateful because it detracts from the unity of mankind. Unity is usually regarded as a spiritual thing, but it can be a material thing, too, since matter in itself is featureless, it being only when it is penetrated by the Logos that qualitative differences arise. Spiritual unity is reached by transcending, and it includes the hierarchical element, but things are brought down to material oneness and that is what is happening today. One of the problems of our time is precisely this materialisation of spirit which involves applying spiritual truths to the material world while neglecting their transcendent origin. The evolutionary goal is for matter to be raised up into spirit as demonstrated at the Ascension of Jesus but today the attempt is made to materialise spirit. Hence the tendency to prioritise quantity, as in egalitarianism, over quality. Spirit cannot be materialised of course, but the mind can seek to do that by inverting the order of being, and that is what is taking place now. Everything is being reduced to the same level, without distinction, a process that, if taken to its natural conclusion, would undo creation and return it to the unqualified homogeneity of the *prima materia*.

This false good also creates for itself a false evil which is anything in which the religion of humanity, together with its central pillar of egalitarianism or oneness, is denied. What the religion of humanity ignores is that being human in the full sense requires seeking the truth of one's being in what is beyond the merely human. If this aspiration or vision of humanity is not allowed, then what happens is this. Instead of rising above the human, one falls below it. Humanity, in this sense, is a staging post not a destination, which is not to diminish it in itself but to see it in its proper context as a kind of focus point in which real spiritual transformation may take place. It seems to be inevitable that if a human being does not seek to transcend himself, he will fall into a lower than human state. Not animal, which is a worthy, natural state, but sub-human. Many of the demons belong to this category.

In the religion of humanity there is a god as there is in all religion. That god is humanity itself and worship is self-worship. But the end goal of this religion lies in the darkness of separation and emptiness as the consequences of this modern variation of idol worship (idol worship being the treating of created things as the Creator) become apparent.

From a spiritual perspective, the most important human faculties are the will and the imagination. In modern man, both of these have been corrupted. The will is no longer oriented to God as it is in a spiritually healthy human being. It points towards self. And the imagination has been crippled by materialism, with the result that the images that feed it are not based on symbols of the divine but, increasingly, those that derive from the infernal regions. Look at so much of modern art, music, film and general culture. Isn't it obvious where this comes from? Imagination now is not called to higher levels of being but spiritual debasement.

The modern age has been marked by the desire to liberate the human will from its 'enslavement' to God, irrationally rejected as irrational. What lies behind this supposed search for freedom is actually egotism, with truth bent to suit the agenda of the autonomous ego. What results is not freedom but increased enslavement to the restrictions of matter. There is no freedom in matter. Without spirit there is only darkness and death. The human imagination has fallen into darkness and can only rise out of that when it opens itself up to transcendent reality. We need as a matter of urgency to re-polarise our will to the truth of God and allow our imagination to receive spiritual light. If imagination is not directed to godly ends it may still be creative, but it will be creatively destructive. This is the sorry path we are on at the moment.

The Contemporary Assault on the Soul

I have spoken of how the current period in history is a kind of gathering in of souls, with the sifting into two main categories of those who are opening up to the light and those who remain closed. It is a real test, the culmination of an age of evolutionary development which has included not just the spiritual but other aspects of our being too. But now is the time that our exam papers must be handed in. The test is made harder by the fact that conditions are bad. Outer factors mitigate against a correct response unless we take it that their very absurdity might drive us in the opposite direction as we react against them. The problem is that many people do not have the long view and do not see how new and greater absurdities are piled on old ones which have become normalised, with the result that the situation is constantly ramped up. We accept what we would have never accepted when in a spiritually healthy state because we have been gradually corrupted over a period of time. Each new corruption is presented as some kind of liberation but, while it may at first be exciting to break boundaries, the liberation is from God and into the loneliness of the separate self. Ultimate freedom in this sense is quite simply nihilism and will lead to despair.

What we are witnessing today is the attempt to expunge any notion of a spiritual component to the human being, one which will lead, if followed through to its natural conclusion, to the complete separation of earthly man and the spiritual realm, to disastrous effect. There may still remain something called religion or spirituality, but it won't be that at all. It will exist simply to reinforce the impregnable edifice of materialism. It will be just another branch of the secular as so many Christian churches have already proved themselves to be. It is now quite obvious that the only way to preserve a real spiritual integrity in the world today is to reject modern ideology *in toto*. If you allow its tenets to enter your mind in any form, they will act like a cancer and spread throughout your whole system. Any concession will bring about eventual submission to the idea that humanism (see previous chapters) overrides the reality of God. This is why such things as feminism, anti-racism and all the other 'isms' are pushed so relentlessly nowadays, with the pushing becoming harder and harder and resistance increasingly depicted as sinful. The whole of modern thought is fundamentally an attack on God and if this wasn't always clear, it surely must be now.

So many modern attitudes are presented as advances in terms of fairness, tolerance, and compassion. Who would want to hold out against such things? But in much the same way that restrictions, supposedly for our own safety, enforced during the coronavirus scare subtly modified human behaviour and psychology on all sorts of levels, so these modern attitudes corrupt our minds on a spiritual level. By focusing on the purely human, using that word to refer solely to human beings materialistically considered, they cut us off from deeper spiritual truths. Which is of course the real intention.

We can tell this by the fact that the process never stops. What seemed innocent enough at first, just the righting of a few historic wrongs, has gathered pace inexorably with more and more truths rooted in the reality of God and Christ either rejected completely or else reformatted to be something quite different. The demands constantly increase and become more extreme. At the same time, what is normal and natural is reinterpreted and shifted to the left, using that word to mean anti-spiritual, which is fundamentally what it does mean and has done since at least the French Revolution, on a near weekly basis, though, there are periods of lull and consolidation and others of strong forward activity. The method employed is constant attack. This is not how truth proceeds. Truth does not attack. It simply presents itself. Evil attacks but good just is itself. This is how we can know, even if it wasn't already quite clear, that the motivation behind the contemporary assault on the mind is evil.

You may find this hard to believe since it is the opposite of perceived reality, but leftism is driven by hate. Ultimately, it is hatred of God but there are many other lesser objects of its hatred, which are usually figures it wants to drag down because of envy and resentment. Eventually, when it runs out of things to tear down, it starts to hate itself, which is why we say, following the journalist and pamphleteer Jacques Mallet du Pan who wrote in 1793 that *"like Saturn, the revolution devours its own children"*, that the revolution ends up eating itself. Hatred needs something to feed on and when it has consumed its enemies it cannot simply stop and rest. It must continue with new enemies.

As the left becomes more extreme a number of well-meaning people on the right mount rear-guard actions. But unless they speak from a real religious point of view they will fail, just as they have over the last few decades. The unholy passion of their opponents is too intense. When all is said and done, the choice is God, with all that implies, or not God. If you have not chosen God, you will fall to the zealots and absorb some of their attitude. The division between those faithful to spiritual truth and the rest will only widen in the coming years. Make sure you are not pulled away from truth by the need to fit in or desire to seem reasonable. Sometimes, if the devil doesn't get souls through hatred he can get them through moral ambivalence or vacillation or even, as it is said, good intentions. He offers poisoned sweets in the form of seemingly fair or on the surface reasonable opinions and attitudes that, if consumed, will end up separating an individual from the truth of Christ. The time is coming when anything that is not actively for Christ will be against him.

* * *

The reader may understandably take exception to my definition
of leftism here, so a few words of explanation are in order.
We can begin by saying that the principles which end up in
the political world as left and right are actually both rooted
in the metaphysical order, where they relate to matter and
spirit. In this sense, they are complementary but there is still
a hierarchical relationship between them. The problem comes
when that relationship is broken, as it is now, when the left is
basically acting as matter trying to usurp the role of spirit. This
is why it has become so powerful in an age in which spirit is
denied and the transcendent ignored. The natural relationship
of complements has turned into a battle between opposites
down in the material world because of metaphysical ignorance
and fallen egos.

Leftism essentially arose in its modern guise when people
gave more importance to this world than the next, and we can
point to the wholly atheist French Revolution as the time it
really took off. Now, even left-wing religious people tend to
see God in terms of Man rather than vice versa as should be the
case. I don't say the right is necessarily spiritual. It very clearly
isn't, especially nowadays, but if it is true to itself and what it is
grounded in, then it should be. In our mixed-up, confused and
rebellious world, you can certainly have a leftist spirituality and
a rightist materialism but this doesn't alter the fact that, taken
back to their metaphysical roots, left and right represent the
material and spiritual poles of existence. That is why the left,
even when it tries to be spiritual, is still essentially God-denying
and heavily contaminated by secular ideology, while the right,
even when it is material, still retains some sense of divine law
and order. It is why the left wants to reduce everything to one,
while the right wants to preserve hierarchical distinction. This
quantitative focus of the left and qualitative focus of the right
reflect their foundation in matter and spirit.

It is sobering to realise that even modern political division is a distant echo of the prime duality of manifestation, albeit at many removes and severely distorted. It is grounded in eternal principles. The right is founded on spirit, unchanging, authoritative, centred in truth and tradition. The left is rooted in matter, concerned with constant change and this world. In a stable society turned towards God these would function as complements, though under the overall headship of the right, centred in divine truth. The problem is that in today's spiritually ignorant world they have become rivals as the right has lost its divine focus and the left seeks to seize and appropriate its position. It is this act of stepping outside its lawful domain that I condemn in the left. But I would also say that a true right is not political at all. It is spiritual and should stand above all politics as the defining background and framework in which these would operate.

Remember the Signs

For many of us, when we come into this world, we are thrown into a place very hard to come to terms with. This is because our source is in the spiritual world which is a realm of beauty, goodness and truth. But this world, beautiful as it is, and it is beautiful because it is the creation of God, is a darkened environment, corrupted by supernatural powers ranged against the light and also by the thoughts and actions of human beings themselves. You may doubt this but the evidence, inner and outer, is irrefutable for anyone alert to spiritual truths.

A large majority allow themselves to be swamped by the world, by 'reality', and generally ignore whatever exists within them that points to a higher reality. Even many supposedly religious people do this, seeing their religion in terms of this world instead of using it to see this world in terms of the light of God. But there are also people who are aware of that light within their own minds, however dim it may be, and decide that this is the light in which they must walk, come what may. They retain a connection, even if that has become but a memory, to their true origin, which is not in this world but a higher one.

The present time is a crisis in the history of humanity. God and his agents have long known of its coming and have prepared for it as much as possible, given that the crisis was inevitable, and they cannot interfere with human free will. The crisis was inevitable because it is partly the result of humanity starting to grow up and become more independent, and that is a good and necessary thing even if the short-term consequences are not good. But it is also inevitable because of the nature of time itself and the fact that it proceeds cyclically. That doesn't mean that things go round in circles because time proceeds historically, linearly, too, but there are cycles within the forward moving direction, and we are coming to the end of one now. It's both the end of a cycle and a definitive point on the line.

For a sensitive soul the current atmosphere, mental and spiritual, is constantly and aggressively attacking the soul. Such a person feels, and even knows, one thing, but everything around him or her pushes in another direction. It can be hard to sustain a connection to truth when practically the whole modern world is against it. One cannot retreat to the past or adopt the spiritual belief system of a different group of humanity which may be less affected by modernity because it is imperative that one is what one is. By that I mean a person's vision must be whole. You are a person living in this place and at this time. Here and now is where you are meant to be. If you try to be something else there will always be an element within you that is being false. You will be divided, and something will not ring true. Spirituality means integrity or it means nothing.

If you can't escape to a time or place other than here and now, what should you do when you find yourself assailed by the world? When you need spiritual support, where do you go? I mean where other than to a religion, but even religion in our day has been captured by the world though its truths remain, of course. But no religion is what it was in terms of its spiritual content and ability to guide or illumine. You may dispute that on a personal level but in general terms I don't see how you can seriously take exception to the statement. Religion is a public institution and all public institutions have been corrupted. This has been an ongoing process over several decades, and maybe even centuries, but the corruption is now so deep that you just can't miss it. This cloud does have a silver lining because it means we are forced back on ourselves and that is as it should be. To become truly spiritual we must be self-reliant, though with the important proviso that we are self-reliant in Christ, not reliant on our own spiritual prowess.

I have taken the title of this chapter from C.S. Lewis's book *The Silver Chair*. It was Aslan's advice to Jill, when he sent her down from his country in the high mountains above the clouds into Narnia to carry out a specific mission. Before he sent her, he gave her certain instructions and pointed to signs she would encounter that would recall her mission when that might escape her attention in the context of dealing with the everyday world. The fact that Jill did not travel down by normal means but by floating through the air indicates a transition from the spiritual to the material realm. She was effectively being born into Narnia and suffered a similar kind of amnesia to the one we experience when we come into this world.

For what happened to Jill happens to us. When are sent out from the higher worlds and born into this one we lose most of our connection to the spiritual plane, though a kind of afterglow remains in the mind during childhood, to a greater or lesser extent depending on the individual. But we have certain impressions stamped on the soul which we need to make the attempt to access. These are the signs from above that we must remember when the world is too much with us. There is a difference in that Jill's signs were all external, whereas we have both external and internal signs to help us negotiate a path through the material world. The internal signs come chiefly through imagination, intuition and conscience. The external signs present themselves to us through religion, myth, legend and the natural world, and some of the great works of art perform a similar function. You might even say that is what makes a great work of art. It's the ability to reflect and recall something of the higher worlds in terms of the beauty and truth of those worlds.

The chief external sign, though, is Jesus. His person represents the point at which heaven opens up to this world. He is a kind of window on heaven and through his word and form we see heaven revealed. You might wonder how this can be so since we only know of Jesus primarily through scripture and then through the church and through art, and none of these are direct, though the gospel of St John might come close.

But I believe that God has enabled a true vision of Jesus to be revealed to humanity through these means. There would not have been much point in Christ coming to Earth if he did not leave a strong impression of himself behind for those who did not encounter him during the short period of his life. Then there is the action of the Holy Spirit, which connects us to the inner Christ. The true figure of Jesus was preserved in the world and he also exists in our heart if we are willing to make the journey to find him.

The whole of creation speaks of its Maker to those who care to look with open eyes, but Jesus Christ is the pre-eminent sign of God in this world and he points straight to the reality of the next one.

The Body is a Frame

It's time to look at a few of the principal lessons we are here to learn while in this world. Some of the lessons are peculiar to ourselves as we each have individual strengths and weaknesses. We don't come to this physical world from nowhere or without baggage. Some of them relate to tasks we must accomplish while here. But some of them are more universal and have to do with knowing ourselves and what we are, and some of these concern how we relate to the environment, for a number of us quite an unnatural one, in which we find ourselves.

I call this an unnatural environment because that is precisely what it is for many people drawn to the spiritual path. Such people have difficulty dealing with material conditions which are much more cramped and restricting than those they recall from a higher level, however dimly that may be. See the previous chapter. For a majority, a statement like this might seem ridiculous but I know what my feelings were about this world and I suspect they are shared by more people than you might think.

A human being is a soul in a body, which term includes the brain. For many people this is not a problem because they don't know the soul so they can just get on with things as they find them. But for a few, who are more polarised towards the spiritual world, it can present a difficulty. Just as a lesson for the majority is to try to become aware of the spiritual component of their being and then bring the material side under the sway of the spiritual, so for some a lesson is to incorporate the material into the spiritual without fear or rejection. The human being must be seen as a whole, though always from above downwards.

One of the traditional problems for the spiritual aspirant is how to relate to the body. In the past some have seen it as an obstacle and the tendency has been to lean too much towards a negation (as much as possible) of the body. Now, we often go too far in the other direction, regarding the body as a fundamental part of what we are, which it is, but it is not *the* fundamental part. I think the words that form the title of this chapter, which were told me by one of my teachers, can be very helpful in giving us a correct perspective in this matter.

First of all, they tell us that our real self is not the body. Many people in the West today would dispute that. Brought up on a diet of scientific materialism, we imagine that the body is what we fundamentally are, and anything else we might seem to be, mind, emotions, even consciousness, derives from that. That is not the Masters' view, nor of course is it the traditional religious view. We are souls in bodies and the body is actually a projection of the soul, not the other way round as present day conventional wisdom would have it.

So, the body is not who or what we are but an outer aspect of who or what we are. In fact, it is a frame. What is the function of a frame? It is to set off a picture. To provide a solid outer structure for the picture and enable it to be displayed. But the picture is the important thing. The frame is not unimportant and it's necessary if you want to hang the picture, but it is not what matters and the picture is just the same without it.

To say that the body is a frame does not in any sense mean one should reject, neglect or not take care of it. After all, no gallery curator would display pictures unworthily with chipped or dirty frames. But it does mean that, although one should look after the body and observe its needs, one should not identify with it or follow its desires. It has its functions, and these are what they are. We should not deny or suppress those we might dislike or fear, but nor should we indulge any of them either. To do the former is to make the body the enemy of the soul and set up a dualistic battle between mind and body. To do the latter increases our identification with the body and its power over us. It separates us from the soul, the proper centre of our being.

Therefore, the course we need to adopt if we wish to realise our true spiritual nature is to treat the body with respect as a divine creation and the medium for our functioning in this world but, at the same time, know it to be only the outermost part of what we are. That means doing what is required to enable the body to act correctly in its role as support for the soul, in terms of diet, exercise, maintaining good health and so on, but not giving it undue prominence or excessive focus or it will usurp attention which should be directed elsewhere. As the Buddha came to appreciate after several years of austerities which led nowhere, a well-cared for physical frame is not a barrier to spiritual understanding but necessary for the mind to have sufficient energy to be able to attend to the spiritual task in hand.

I called the body a divine creation and so I believe it to be. The Master in the passage from which I extracted this chapter's heading, included in full in the appendix, spoke of its having been designed, and I consider him a knowledgeable authority in this matter. That the body is designed is my intuitive feeling also and intuition is important. However, this does not mean I fall into the creationist camp. With regard to the human form, I understand this to have originally existed in the spiritual world, somewhat similar to a Platonic archetype, and then been realised, as best it may, given the resistance of physical matter to spiritual impulse, over a period of time. Pre-existing forms may well have been adapted to bring forth the human form, but I don't see even these animal forms as entirely arbitrary. Again, the spiritual idea precedes the material form, but these also develop and change through currently accepted evolutionary means. In other words, the form of incarnated beings comes about through a mixture of spiritual ideation and evolution as it is understood from the modern scientific perspective. I would place the primary impulse on the spiritual side and regard evolution more as a tweaking mechanism which might develop new and interesting variations on an archetypal theme.

What this means is that the gulf between those who believe in a spiritual origin and design of the human body and those who see the body, indeed the whole human being, as coming about through random mutations and 'survival of the fittest' can only be crossed when each side accepts that the truth contains elements of the insights of the other as well as their own. Neither is sufficient by itself. I would certainly place the emphasis on spiritual principles guiding the process overall but what you might call the unconscious or material side also plays a part in the development of form, by no means as big a part as presently surmised, but an important part nonetheless. For those who think that this is hedging my bets, I can only say that when human beings take diametrically opposed positions on a subject the truth often falls between the two, or perhaps transcends them both, including them but seen from a higher perspective. Moreover, if we regard manifesting life as the product of the creative interplay between spirit and matter then it is reasonable to suppose that both of these polarities must have an influence on the end result. However, as should be obvious, the origin of human bodies is of secondary importance, given that we are not bodies but souls and these are of purely spiritual origin.

We are living in a material world, encased in a material form, and it can be hard to detach ourselves from that and realise that the latter is just an outer aspect or frame. And yet I truly believe that we can know ourselves to be souls by listening to the voice in the heart, which is always present though often drowned out by external noise and commotion coming from our own thoughts, prejudices and opinions, as well as those that prevail in the society in which we live. The truth is ever-present, accessible to all not just a minority of esoteric adventurers or the spiritually gifted. We can reject that truth, deny it, rebel against it for whatever reason, but it will remain, and the truth is that human beings are spiritual beings currently experiencing life in matter for reasons pertaining to the development of consciousness. The body in which they find themselves, and with which they may confuse themselves, is but a frame, by no means to be identified with but to be used and respected as a vehicle or support for the manifestation of what they truly are which is spiritual consciousness, individual centres of love, intelligence and creativity.

But there is a final important point, the body may be a frame in the context of the totality of what we are but a human being is formed from the marriage of spirt and matter. As far as we know, we are unique in that respect. This means we are not just spiritual consciousness but spiritual consciousness with form. We may lose our physical body when we die but I believe that the ascension of Christ demonstrated that we will have a heavenly body which, we can speculate, will be made of transubstantiated matter, spiritualised matter, matter converted into light. Christ showed us that it is not just the soul that is saved. Ultimately, the body is too. The frame will remain part of the picture.

Subdue the Mind

"At present your moods veer from high to low and you are at the mercy of your thoughts. You must keep on an even keel and remain balanced at all times. When antagonistic thoughts or negative emotions arise you should breathe in, palms outstretched, imagining God's purifying rays entering your mind. As you exhale, imagine all the bad influences departing. Do this ten times and strive to subdue the mind."

I don't suppose any but the greatest saints are completely free of antagonistic thoughts and negative emotions. I was given this instruction 40 years ago and it's something I still need to work on. To achieve this is one of the great lessons of the earthly school because what it really requires is the ability to break the identification with the mind and know yourself to be the soul. To recognise this intellectually is one thing. To know it fully, quite another.

If we are not the body then neither are we the mind, not the thought-making, ego-centred mind which is our day to day focus. This is part of our mortal self, the material side of our being, and bound up with living and working in the outer world of things. It can speculate about the higher worlds but only from the outside looking in. The higher worlds can only be known when we move beyond the thinking mind to the cognitive function that belongs to these worlds, which is intuition. Intuition is a soul faculty that approaches knowledge from the inside, the point at which being and knowing coincide. The precursor to intuition, the door that leads to it, is faith. Faith, which is a quite different thing to belief, is the opening of the mind to what is beyond it.

My conception of the spiritual anatomy of a human being is that it is threefold. Spirit, soul and body. In this formulation, spirit is the divine part of our being, the part where we and God are essentially one, soul is the spiritual part, meaning the locus of our individuality and personal identity, and body, also threefold, consists of the part we are most aware of in the world, our mind, emotional nature and the physical body itself. Some call this the lower self, with the soul as higher self and spirit as divine self. Obviously, this is just a representation of a deep mystery, but I believe it bears a reasonable approximation to the truth.

What it tells us is that if we wish to come close to our spiritual self and function from that level, we must learn to **subdue the mind.** This means detach ourselves from identification with the thinking self as well as the emotional self (**remain balanced**) and the physical body. Being detached from emotions does not mean not allowing yourself to feel, any more than being detached from thought means not thinking. It means not allowing emotions to dominate you and not responding to **negative emotions** whether these be feelings of anger and antipathy or any one of the many manifestations of what the Master calls in the extract above, moods. Note that he also talks about moods veering from high to low and how this should be avoided. This tells us that it is not only negative emotions that we should learn to overcome or master. It is any kind of emotional excess which indicates that we are functioning on the level of personal feelings and craving, seeking satisfaction for the me, the earthly ego. Essentially, we should avoid feelings but cultivate feeling.

Meditation is a traditional way to subdue the mind, but I do not recommend meditation in a secular context as is fashionable these days. This might still the thought-making movement of the mind and give the practitioner a sense of peace, even bliss, but it will not take him beyond the mind to the true spiritual plane, not on its own. In the spiritual world everything is determined by motivation and orientation of the heart. There is no method or technique that will bring about a spiritual transformation, even if some methods might seem to do that to those who equate anything out of the ordinary of a psychological nature as spiritual. This is not the case. There are many levels of the mind between the physical and the true spiritual and these are clearly specified in the mystical writings of most religions. You can subdue the outer mind but still be caught up in one of the inner layers of the mind if your attitude to God and the higher world is contaminated by self-seeking desire. This is why I was told by my teachers that meditation was good, but I also needed the humbling experience of prayer. Meditation directs us to God Immanent if practised right, but God is Transcendent, too, and if you fail to acknowledge that you will remain at the level of self even if that self appears to have been "spiritualised".

Perhaps at one time it was reasonable for people to start meditating outside of a religious context, but I believe that time has passed. Now, in the present spiritual state of the world, it leans towards self-indulgence and dilettantism, spirituality as lifestyle. It can even be spiritually unhealthy if you think you are actually leading some kind of spiritual life but are neglecting God. You may be creating an imaginary world for yourself in your meditation or spiritual practice, a world the appearance of which may be spiritual, but the animating presence is materialistic. That's to say, based on the desires and satisfactions of the worldly self. Many people take their worldly attitudes into their search for the next world but only if your focus is truly spiritual will your discoveries and encounters be spiritual as well.

All of which brings me to the best way to subdue the earthly mind. It is much easier, and perhaps this is the only true way, to overcome something through a positive replacement of that thing than through the attempt to control and master. It may then just happen naturally and without effortful struggle which, as we know from traditional Buddhist teaching, tends to perpetuate the very thing it seeks to dominate. Where the mind is concerned, that is rather like trying to make yourself taller by standing on your head. From this perspective, the best way to subdue the mind and the ego and, in fact, the whole self-centred, earthly personality is through learning to subordinate these to something greater than all of them and that is the love of God.

When it comes down to it, this is the most important lesson to be learned in the whole of life. Everything else is peripheral, both materially and spiritually. Love of God, the intuitive recognition of and opening up of the heart to the Creator, is the key to everything. It is certainly the key to heaven.

Here is a paradox. You must be virtuous to get to heaven, but the virtuous man does not go to heaven. All civilisations worthy of the name acknowledge the law which is right behaviour or what C.S. Lewis in his short but important work *The Abolition of Man* called the Tao. This is the correct way to act with regard to the gods, the universe and one's fellow man. Details may vary but the essentials are remarkably similar everywhere. And yet this is not enough. Observing the Ten Commandments will not get you to heaven. Neither will do as you would be done by. The Pharisees do not go to heaven and this is true even of the good Pharisees not just the ones who observe the letter of the law but neglect its spirit.

The only thing that will get you to heaven is the love of God. Nothing you can do, nothing you can think, no belief you have, no moral rules you follow will get you to heaven, but handing yourself over to God in absolute faith and trust and love will. That is because this love is the only thing that will cure the stain of ego which blocks our entry into heaven. This great truth was demonstrated for us by Jesus at the Crucifixion, which was a kind of outer representation of an inner spiritual journey that all must take eventually who wish to be spiritually resurrected.

Good people do not go to heaven. Consider that for a moment. They remain themselves, untransformed, spiritually unborn.

Don't think this is an impossible task. God is always there, waiting to respond to any overture we might make. Even a little attempt to love on our part. All we have to do is turn towards him in truth and humility and he will respond. There will still remain much work to be done because the ego self, the swollen self-regarding me, is very powerful but once love for God has risen in our heart then we are facing in the right direction. In fact, even the recognition that we lack this love and the sincere desire to acquire it is an important first step in the purification of the self and its preparation for eventual entry into the Kingdom of Heaven.

I'll tell you the reason for this. It's just common sense really. Love of God shows that you actually recognise and want what heaven is. If you don't even want it, how can you expect to go there?

Therefore, learn to subdue the mind, which is the centre of your earthly self and that which blocks your progress from this world to the higher ones. Do not neglect to develop the mind. It is part of the totality of what you are, and all aspects of your being should reach their highest potential. This, too, is one of the earthly lessons. But know that there will come a point when your mind becomes your enemy and will need to be conquered. Love of God is the best way to do this. Then the mind will become a friend again, a good servant you can rely on to carry out the will of the soul.

Jesus Christ and the Mysteries

It has sometimes been remarked that key episodes in the life of Jesus can be taken as symbolising stages on the spiritual path for any true disciple. This goes along with the idea that Jesus's life was an externalisation or enactment of the ancient mysteries, those rituals that initiated the qualified candidate into the realities of the spiritual world, originally through the offices of sage-priests in touch with that world but in later, more degenerate times, through drugs as the spiritual quality of both priest and candidate dropped and the materialisation of the environment reached the point at which the windows between the physical plane and higher ones became more opaque. I once visited the King's Chamber of the Great Pyramid and was fortunate enough to be left there by myself for a while. Alone in the silence, it seemed obvious that this was a place of ritual in which the neophyte would experience death and rebirth while lying in the stone sarcophagus that is the only object there. This was the core of the ancient mysteries. It was a dramatic ritual for the Egyptian initiate but performed literally by Christ as he revealed the hidden secret of life and made potentially accessible to everyone what had been open, and only partially open at that, to an elite few before.

The life of Christ can give us a deep understanding of the spiritual path that we too must tread before we are worthy to join him as resurrected beings in his heavenly kingdom. I will examine seven major episodes from his life but there will be more that can teach us new things about ourselves for it is a truism that a study of Christ's life can be endlessly revelatory.

Here are the seven episodes I see as crucial stages to be passed by the aspiring disciple on his way to eternal life. There follows my interpretations of these stages but each one of them will richly reward further meditation, which is a traditional spiritual exercise. These are the final lessons that come to us in the earthly school.

His Birth.

The obvious beginning. Christ must be born in our heart. This doesn't just mean becoming a Christian for that can be merely an external affair. It means we acknowledge the reality of Christ as the truth in the light of which all other truths must be seen. We accept his reality as the foundation of everything and resolve at the deepest level of our being to coordinate our soul to that. This is clearly an aspiration. We are a long way off from realising it and will stumble and fall many times, but a sincere start has been made. We have reoriented our self from a focus on this world and its goals to the higher spiritual world. I don't say this has specifically to be directed at the historical figure of Jesus Christ but, if it is within the parameters of any other spiritual approach, it should be directed towards something that echoes and holds at least part of the reality of Christ. The highest form of spiritual reality, of truth, beauty and goodness we can conceive of at the moment.

Preaching in the Temple.

This is a moment at which we have made some progress on the spiritual path and are able to share something of what we have learned. It may not be at a very elevated stage. Jesus was only 12 after all. But it will still be better than the worldly wisdom of the "Doctors" who may represent the professionals of outer teaching.

Baptism.

At this point we are brought into closer contact with the soul or higher self. This is the part of us that exists on the spiritual level, above that of the everyday mind which we normally assume to be the centre of what we are, and which is the source of intuition.

It is the real beginning of being guided by this spiritual sense and going beyond the threefold lower self, associated with the physical, emotional and mental worlds. We now know our self as the soul, something that until this point we have had intimations of but not been able to fully centre our self in. We still can't do that, but a point has been reached at which the balance of power has definitely shifted and the baby Christ within us has reached some kind of maturity. Clearly, many people might think they have reached this stage before they have because their intellectual understanding of the soul has outstripped their ability really to be it. This is one of the pitfalls to be negotiated by the disciple, both in respect of himself and in respect of others, outer teachers, to whom he might wish to give spiritual allegiance. I don't think this stage on the spiritual path has much to do with the religious ritual of baptism. That is a symbolic echo of it at an earlier point in the cycle.

Temptation in the Wilderness.

Once you have reached a certain stage of spiritual development you will be tested to see if you can maintain that in the face of appeals to egotism. Tests and trials are an ongoing feature of the spiritual life, but this is now serious stuff. You have attained a certain level of real knowledge. What effect does that have on you? Does it fuel pride? Is there a temptation to use it for your own ends? Or do you humbly accept the responsibility of it, seeing it not as your possession but as a gift from God, a gift that could be withdrawn should you react to it as your own? The significance of this stage should be obvious. It is perhaps the culmination of all the previous tests, with the aim of giving you a clean bill of spiritual health. But it has echoes at many earlier stages of the spiritual path. Tests are one of the more important elements of the earthly school, as they are of normal schools, and one to which we should be constantly alert.

Transfiguration.

I interpret this as the moment we become fully aligned with the soul. We are now, as it were, the soul in embodiment. The spiritual self illuminates the whole being of the threefold lower self which become vehicles of expression rather than centres in their own right. Obviously, this is a stage in theosis, well beyond most of us at present but it can be seen in the lives of some of the saints. Our being is irradiated by spiritual light. The process that came into full view at the baptism reaches a culmination. Christ in us has reached full maturity.

Crucifixion

It is interesting that this previous stage is not the conclusion of the path. We seem to have reached the pinnacle of spiritual achievement. We have climbed to the top of the mountain. What can there be left to do? However, there is something more. We have to give it all up. All the hard-won spiritual success must be renounced, for it is only by doing this that our motive can really be seen to be true. We give back to God all he has given to us, thereby showing that it is love of God that has driven us forward, not the quest for some kind of personal reward. We are prepared to sacrifice all we have attained to prove our dedication to God. This is what Christ showed in the Garden of Gethsemane. "Not my will but Thine be done". This is what it all comes down to: the full renunciation of self. But please note this is not the seeing through of the illusion of self as in some forms of spirituality. Self is real. The crucifixion is agony. It is not some kind of peaceful transition to bliss. There is the sense of real and total sacrifice. There was for Christ and there will be for us, though it will probably be in the nature of an existential crisis rather than a physical one. For Jesus it was clearly both, but that was because of the nature of his mission.

Resurrection

After the supreme sacrifice comes glory. The risen Christ. The soul loses everything, or apparently does. But it must give up everything, and this is not done with one eye on the prize. It really seems to be spiritual abandonment and darkness, but after death there is rebirth. The soul is remade as a completely spiritualised being, an individualisation of God himself. It is the entry into the fifth kingdom of life, that of immortal souls. For immortality up to this point has been conditional. Now it has been completely won and there is no return. The resurrection of Christ marks the fulfilment of life and the return of the soul to its Creator, but this time with full knowledge. The circle is complete.

* * *

These are the mysteries of Jesus Christ, demonstrated in his life, which also, I believe, actually made them possible of achievement for human beings. He was the trailblazer who through his life and death connected the physical world to the spiritual, bringing them both together and opening up a channel between the two. He created a path that now anyone following after may walk if they so wish – and are prepared to make the necessary sacrifice for. Just because it is possible does not mean it is easy. But it is possible, and we can do it with Christ as our guide for he is the Head Master of the earthly school.

Why Did the New Age Movement Fail?

One of the premises of this book is that the popular belief that all religions say roughly the same thing, being man's attempts to express the numinous in different ways since no one way can have a monopoly on the truth, is incorrect. Christ and the truth he brought really are qualitatively different to anything else. He is the face and form of God in a way nothing else is and he offers a truth and a salvation no one and nothing else can. Other religions are perfectly valid on their own terms and in terms of what they claim to offer but they are not reflections of the Most High in the same way that Christianity is. They can provide a path to inner dimensions of creation, whether that be as regards consciousness or paradise, but they do not all bring one to the beatific vision of the Creator though theistic religions that describe union with God are close. In these, Christ may be spiritually present even if not in his outer represented form.

That doesn't mean that Christianity nowadays in any of its institutional forms is what is required. At this time all institutions are corrupt and none pure, and this is true for the Christian ones as well. We are now called to find truth within ourselves and be self-guided rather than rely on anything external. At the same time, our self-guidance must come from a place beyond the self to be authentic, and it must also be governed by the light of Christ. I am speaking from the perspective of a Westerner. Eastern religions have their own path, though even in those there must be some illumination from Christ if they are to be effective. This will not be expressed in the form of Christ but should be inhabited by his presence. And speaking of form, that is the reason why Eastern religions are not suitable, generally speaking, for Westerners. They come from a different time and place. We can learn from Eastern religions, I certainly have, but they are usually an ill-fitting suit for the Western body. The converse may be true as well even if Christ himself is universal.

I bring all this up because I want to speak a little about the New Age movement. Was this just spiritual sensationalism or was there some point to it? Was it a genuine development of spiritual understanding as it believed itself to be or was it a deviation that led astray? Let us enquire.

Whether the revival of interest in mysticism, esotericism and the occult that fell under the umbrella term of the New Age, roughly lasting from the 1960s to the end of the millennium, was something that was at one time divinely inspired which went awry because of a failure to live up to its ideals or whether it was just a response to natural cycles or maybe an attempt by dark powers to divert spiritual aspiration into psychic channels, one would have to say it was not a success in terms of fostering real spirituality. For some people it might have been an inspiration to higher things but only if they went beyond it as it was in itself, using it as a springboard to greater understanding and leaving it behind like milk to meat in St Paul's analogy. But there is no doubt that in itself and its attitude to the spiritual world, it was shallow and self-indulgent.

The New Age was born from two things. The descent of religion into dull conventionalism and outer observance, and the increasing desire of a substantial minority to experience something of the reality that was thought to be behind the original religious impulse. I have no doubt that the widespread consumption of psychedelic drugs fed into the process too. The whole thing was given a boost by the increasing availability of spiritual books written from the perspective of a variety of traditions and also the exposure to Eastern religion of large numbers of people. This had all happened before, coincidentally or not, during the same decades at the end of the 19th century, and then to a limited extent and only amongst the intelligentsia in the 1920s. But at the end of the 20th century it was more widespread and open to most sections of society.

The keyword of the New Age would be experience. People wanted spiritual experience. This is fine up to a point. Personal experience can give an individual greater insight into the structure of reality and confirm what religion only teaches about. But the important thing about experience is the experiencer. Why is he seeking experience and what does he do with it once it has passed? Does he seek to repeat it for the pleasure he gets from it (even if he calls that 'bliss') or does he use it to learn more about himself and the world? If the latter, what sort of things is he looking for? Knowledge, power, higher consciousness? This was the primary problem with the New Age. It attracted people to higher things who were motivated by their lower nature and it did not do enough to discourage that, or instruct its adherents in the proper traditional ways of spiritual development, particularly when it came to the purification of the aforementioned lower nature.

People were in it for what they could get out of it. That is not a good approach to the spiritual path which should be based on the love of God. It is also an approach that can be easily exploited by the demonic powers and there is little doubt that whatever else the New Age may have been, a not insignificant part of it was or became demonically inspired.

The New Age emphasised immanence over transcendence. As a corrective to past over-emphasis on transcendence this was good, but it had a fatal flaw. The focus on human potential and subsequent demotion of God left it exposed to self-absorption and narcissism. Instead of being truly spiritual it became largely therapeutic, concerned with feelings and sensations, with methods and practises designed to boost happiness in the present moment and reduce the 20th century materialistic sense of alienation. But, like drunkards always seeking the next bottle when the effects of the last one wore off, this meant New Age enthusiasts joined a merry-go-round of spiritual adventurism, healers, chakra boosting workshops, the whole circus, and there were always plenty of salesmen to cater to that. The trouble with a religion based on feelings and chasing 'bliss' is that there is always a law of diminishing returns and you get caught up in your own desires, the very reverse of a true spiritual attitude which Jesus summed up in "Take up your cross and follow me". There was no cross in the New Age and no sense of inherent sin. Instead it was centred on the aims and aspirations of the human being as a human being. It may have talked about transcending the ego but if it's the ego itself who is behind this then you are not going to get very far. There is also the problem that when you prioritise the immanent nature of divinity you fall into the ludicrous trap of believing that you make your own reality. There is no real objective truth to which you have to coordinate your being. Reality can be what you want it to be. This was another widespread illusion associated with New Age thought.

This dismantling of the objective nature of reality was a major contributory factor for the strong correlation there is between the New Age and leftism, with its Utopian idealism based on bending truth to ideology. It also partially explains why the New Age was so easily corrupted by the sexual revolution, not seeing any real conflict between sex and spirituality or even regarding the two as somehow interlinked so you can have such travesties as sacred sexuality with no recognition of the inherent absurdity of such a thing. That's because there is a relationship between sex and spirituality in that they involve the same energy but going in different directions. Either up to head and heart or down to the sexual centres. Just as water cannot run in two directions at the same time in the same river nor can the creative energy. This doesn't mean celibacy is required for spiritual aspirants but control and the submission of lust to love certainly is.

And there is one final and serious flaw in most New Age spirituality. This is the absence of Christ who is either ignored altogether or just reduced to a spiritual teacher, one among many, teaching higher consciousness like a guru. For us in the West (and maybe elsewhere, but the New Age was a Western thing), genuine spiritual transformation, call it salvation, is only possible through the Logos as incarnated, spiritually as well as physically, in Christ. There are other forms of spirituality but none that actually save the soul in the sense of redeeming it from this world, which term I use to include the psychic dimensions that surround the physical realm just as much as the physical realm itself.

In many ways the New Age was a return to pre-Christian forms of religion but there is a big problem with that. These forms, call them paganism, served a purpose in the time before Christ but Christ's advent changed everything. The necessary approach to spirituality changed, which is why you cannot go back. Christ really did bring something different and new and better and all earlier religions were put in his shade. They had served their purpose, but they now lacked something vital and became effectively atavistic. The institutional shortcomings of the Christian religion are well-known, but its essence remains as true as ever and there is nothing else that can substitute for it. And there is no substitute for Christ. The New Age ignored this, which is the primary reason for its failure.

My Kingdom is Not of This World

If we were looking for some kind of scriptural support for the idea that Earth is a school which does not exist in and for itself, we might find it in a saying of Jesus from the gospel of St John. This gospel, by the way, has a convincing claim to contain the most profound spiritual teaching to be found anywhere. That extends beyond the actual teaching to the form, the very words, even in translation, especially for English speakers the King James version, in which it is presented. This little book carries the imprint of the higher worlds. It is bathed in a light and clarity from beyond this mortal sphere. All four gospels present different sides to Jesus so we get a more rounded picture of him than we might do from one alone, but it is John who sees most deeply into the inner Christ.

"My kingdom is not of this world." Jesus uses these words when being questioned by Pilate, and he follows them with something else that is not often commented on. He says, *"If it were, my servants would fight to prevent my arrest by the Jews."* The Jews here stand for the worldly powers, something like Caesar in an earlier confrontation with the Pharisees. I believe the point Jesus makes tells us, we who would follow in the footsteps of his disciples, not to mix religion, which is of the spiritual world, and politics which is of this one. When religion descends to politics, it becomes politics and ceases to be religion, which doesn't mean the religious person should ignore politics but he should not allow himself to get mixed up in it. If you do, you will be assimilated by it. Was that not perhaps the mistake Judas made?

I make this point because our world is increasingly going to descend into madness. That's what always happens when its roots to the spiritual are severed. The temptation for right thinking people who see this, and watch horrified as lies and deceit run riot throughout society, will be to fight the madness through political means. But they will fail and end up angry and embittered. The die is cast. The process towards a certain end is inexorable. This world is heading towards the installation of the figure known as the Antichrist at its head. But while we cannot prevent that we should certainly resist it in our hearts and there may indeed come a time, as it came for the early Christians, when we have to take some kind of a stand. But it should all be in the name of God not as an attempt to preserve something we value in this world. Many years ago, my teachers told me this. **"Your fears of losing what you feel inside are groundless. Nothing good, nothing true can ever be lost."** It can disappear in this world, but it can never be lost in the place it comes from which is the higher world and it will always exist there ready to manifest itself again in happier earthly times.

To fight the decline is valiant and it's good that people do it and do not let the worldly powers have everything their own way. But for those who believe in God this must be done from the spiritual plane. We should sound the alarm and proclaim the truth, but the real battle is, as it always is, within our own soul. It's all too easy to be distracted away from that and fight evil externally, but this means you will be drawn into evil. Go down to its level, meet it on its own ground, and you will be absorbed into its snares. No doubt this is one of the meanings of Christ's advice not to resist evil. Fight it within yourself. Reveal it when you see it but don't try to use its own weapons against it. It thrives by confrontation. Once again, we can look to the example of Christ who did not argue or debate when tried but simply was what he was.

The fact that Christ's kingdom is not of this world is why all Utopian idealists are actually working against him and for the other fellow – whether they know it or not, and most don't, but even so that's no excuse. It is obviously not wrong to try to make the world a better place but it should be understood that this is always just a short-term thing, destined to ultimate failure. Absolute good can never be established in this world because of the nature of the human being. Our free will means there will always be a proclivity to sin. True and lasting goodness can only be realised in God. There is no perfect earthly society and is not meant to be. There are certainly some societies that try, more or less successfully, to reflect the pattern of the heavens, ancient Egypt, ancient India, medieval Christendom are good examples of that, but all these have flaws and come to an end. Earth is a school and will remain so for as long as it exists in its present form.

School Teachers

A regular school can only be considered as such if it has teachers and the pupils know they are in class. That is not the case with this school. There are certainly spiritual teachers plying their trade in the world but that is not what I mean. The idea of a spiritual teacher as opposed to priests and monks is a relatively new conception in the West (India has had gurus for centuries of course) and I'm not sure how useful they are. Many of them seem to adopt the profession, if I can call it that, as a way to perpetuate their spiritual life which might otherwise lack stimulation. The sad truth is that to be regarded as a beacon of wisdom and compassion is a pretty intoxicating brew that is likely to go to the head of all but the sturdiest soul. And what do spiritual teachers do exactly? I'm not talking about those functioning within the context of a religion or novice masters in monasteries or even preachers, but the freelance teachers who present themselves as enlightened and offer to guide others to enlightenment. They might help in introducing neophytes to key spiritual concepts and basic practices but other than that one is inclined to think that many of them exist for the furtherance of themselves. Perhaps that is an ungenerous generalisation, but the last 50 years has seen a lot of this sort of thing, much of it linked with various aspects of the New Age – see previous chapter.

Anyway, the lessons of the earthly school are much broader than simple spiritual training. All aspects of our being are catered for and our lessons come through our experiences in life rather than from sitting down in class. We don't even have to know they are taking place to benefit from them, though that might make the process seem long and slow. But then, they do have to seep in right to the depths of our being. It is not mere mind knowledge we are talking about here. So, from this point of view, the teacher is life. Really, it's God, but we can best see his action as it operates through life. When Jesus said that not one sparrow falls to the ground without God knowing, he was referring back to this idea. God is present in everything.

God has to manifest his action without us being aware of it because the nature of this school requires us to believe in the full reality of what happens to us and what we do. If we knew that there was a large element of artifice in our worldly lives, in that we do have a certain destiny and that there is a general organisation behind our lives, we would be too detached from our lessons and not learn from them. This is why there is just enough evidence of God for those who want to believe in him but not quite enough for those who don't. If you think about it, this delicate balance is extraordinarily clever and actually a strong hint for the reality of God. But that will only convince those who want to believe.

I am not saying this world is an illusion. Our lives are fully real and our actions have consequences. Our freedom is at all times paramount. But there is still a degree in which we are actors in a play. We have our parts but can improvise many of our lines.

Apart from life in general, our teachers are the people we meet and the close relationships we form. One of the drawbacks of the monastic life, in other respects ideal for spiritual development especially that of a contemplative nature, is that you are restricting your personal relationships. Opportunities for service and sacrifice and tests come through such relationships. Marriage and family life offer an excellent arena for spiritual growth. They can be loving and creative and help one to forget oneself and live for others, but they can also be full of hardship and suffering, pain, confrontation and difficulty. However, this too can bear spiritual fruit if one responds to it correctly. Like it or not, tests, trials and tribulations are an important part of the earthly schooling. They come to everyone but certainly increase the further along the path one proceeds.

When a person reaches a certain stage on the spiritual path, that person is going to be tested. Those who think that once you decide to follow a spiritual course your life will be full of love, peace and joy have little idea of the reality of things. The point of spirituality is not to make the lower, earthly self happy in the here and now but to burn out the fires of ego, and that is not a pleasant operation. True spirituality is putting yourself in God's hands and letting him do what he wants with you in the certain knowledge that what he wants is the good of your soul, and that might include temporary and short-term suffering. Actually, I can go further. It definitely will include that. Moreover, the further you proceed in real spirituality, the more suffering you are likely to encounter. This can be physical, some of the saints have endured dreadful ill health, but it is perhaps more likely to be mental and take a form that those still ensnared in this world simply can't understand. All this is designed to extract you from attachments to your own selfish egotism. And don't most of us take to spirituality for at least partially selfish motives?

As we progress along the path, our integrity is tested. False motivations are brought out and must be jettisoned. Our goals are questioned, and we are asked whether we can sacrifice personal happiness for love. It would be nice if we could be sure that this was what was happening when it was happening, that a test was only a test, but that would mitigate the lesson and often we are kept completely in the dark. God is not there when we call on him. Any spiritually pleasant feelings of expansion we may have experienced at one time are cut off. We are thrown back on our self with no outer or inner support at all. We must just press on in faith and hope that one day the clouds will clear. Which they will, but there's no telling when.

This is all part of the test we must undergo to become spiritually perfect. Just think about that phrase for a moment. Spiritually perfect. That is our goal. Could it possibly be an easy thing of accomplishment? It must be the hardest thing there is because it is the crowning achievement of any human being in this world. It really does require the sacrifice of the earthly self, and that is never going to be a simple matter. It wasn't for the saints, and it won't be for us.

But there is something else over and above this spiritual testing. The Masters told me that the further anyone goes on the spiritual path, the more they will be attacked by dark forces and I have definitely observed this to be so. It takes various forms. It can be internal attack as these powers seek to gain purchase in your mind by influencing your thoughts and feelings in certain directions. Or it can be external when you find yourself under attack by people you know, people you might come into contact with or even people with whom you might be close.

Now, it's very important to be sensible about this, to maintain a sense of proportion and avoid feelings of paranoia, thinking that anyone who disagrees with you is being manipulated by dark forces. You might be the one who is in the wrong. Nevertheless, it is the case that often those who are doing God's work in some way, or even just striving to live a life in accordance with spiritual truth, are attacked and undermined by others. These people may have their own agenda but they might also be taken advantage of by the demons, though this would not be possible if the demons were not able to find a point of entrance in the person's soul through which they could gain access. They can only work with what is already there.

Some of the forms that attacks commonly take are unjust accusations and lies about your moral character. These can often be very cunningly delivered with truth twisted just enough to make them almost plausible. Chinks in your armour are constantly sought, and faults you may actually possess are exaggerated and given excessive emphasis. It's as though darkness hates light and wants to drag it down to its own level, which it does by accusing it of its own faults. The well-known phenomenon of projection is often in evidence, in which the accuser berates the accused for behaving in the way that it, the accuser, is behaving. The devil has a serpentine mind and twists and turns in a manner that can be quite confusing to a spiritual person who, generally speaking, is someone who leans towards simplicity. That's because truth is simple. It's truth and that's all there is to it. But lies are always devious, and the devil is a particularly skilled liar and distorter. Those he influences behave in the same way.

What's the best way to defend yourself against this kind of attack? If possible, break off contact with the person, but if that is not possible, try not to respond in kind. That's what the dark powers want. They want to drag you down. It may be that you have some kind of spiritual connection to the person who attacks you and it is your task to experience this and see it out. Those who believe in reincarnation might see this as a karmic thing, but even those who don't should be able to see that even this form of attack can be an opportunity for you to learn to rise above the abuse and miscomprehension of this world. God might even use unjust attacks on you as a means of teaching you non-reaction and detachment. It's easy to get indignant if you are unjustly abused or your good name is tarnished, but you have to learn that God sees the truth and that's all that matters. If you are a villain in the eyes of the world what does that matter if God knows the reality? Ultimately, the desire to be thought well of comes from the ego. It may be that you have to learn to let go of everything, including what past generations would have called your honour.

Tests and trials are all part of the spiritual life. We must be prepared for them and not be surprised if we are attacked by anti-spiritual forces sworn to an agenda of destruction. Even those tribulations that comes from demons are used by God to further his plan. That is not to justify them, but God can use them to help us grow in spiritual strength and insight. Being put in danger is a bad thing but how else are you going to learn courage? There's no danger in heaven and there's no evil there either, of course, but heaven requires its inhabitants to have been tested in the fire and shown their mettle.

We may not see our teachers or even be aware that we have such, but they are there. Every one of us has a guide of some sort on higher levels of being. I am not talking about guardian angels. I have no personal experience of these, though I don't doubt they exist. But I do have some experience of teachers from the spiritual planes and can say a bit about that.

My teachers were a group of souls who had achieved oneness with God. At various times they described themselves as his messengers and they clearly were qualified in that respect. I talk about their mode of communication in the appendix, so here I will just speak a little about them as they were or seemed to me to be. To begin with, though they were a group who spoke and appeared to think all in complete unity or, better put, harmony, they were fully individual. I could tell one from another even though I never actually saw any of them other than through their medium whose face, when overshadowed, did sometimes acquire a great nobility that, with all due respect to him, he did not have in normal life. But then no one does. However, their absorption into the life of God had in no way diminished their human qualities. Rather, it had raised these to a kind of perfection in which egotism and the tendency to sin had totally disappeared while all good things we associate with humanity remained. They were indeed men made perfect and demonstrated this in the degree of love and wisdom they manifested in their dealings with me. Neither of these characteristics presented themselves in the detached, impersonal way you sometimes associate with the sage or spiritual superman. Their love was not expressed as a universalised, all-purpose compassion but was fully personal. It wasn't just that they were loving but that they loved me, which I say not with the assumption that I was worthy of that love but to show its quality.

Their wisdom and understanding of human nature was faultless. They certainly understood me, and their instructions bore this out. They could see into my heart without questioning me and appeared to know everything about my life and, from what they said, not only my current life. As with their love, their wisdom was not abstract generalisation but practical, specific, always to the point and never vague. They neither sought praise nor required any kind of obedience, except that owed by a spiritual student to his teacher without which the student cannot learn. This was certainly not a relationship of equals, but I had complete freedom.

I say they were not all the same and they weren't, and it is interesting to note that in heaven full individuality is preserved, enhanced, in fact, and also that the opportunity for spiritual progress deeper into the heart of God continues. My teachers spoke of those beyond them whom they called higher Masters and on a few occasions I was spoken to by these beings. It was like being in the presence of a mighty mountain.

I don't think we all have spiritual teachers of this kind but we do all have guides who are there to help us negotiate our way through life insofar as they can, which is probably quite limited with regard to outer things but more pronounced where spiritual matters are concerned. But we have to know how to speak to them and how to hear them. We speak to them through prayer and the opening of the heart and mind in their direction. Ask and it shall be given, though it is not always given in an obvious way or the one you might expect. We don't pray to them of course, but we can talk to them, question them and ask for their help. Humility and faith are important as they always are in the spiritual world.

We hear them through the intuition. I was told by my teachers that they sought to impress ideas on me. This will be done at the level of the higher mind and we have to become receptive to that mind, which we can do by suppressing brain chatter and focusing on the mind in the heart. Contemplation is a key method for doing this but to be spiritually effective contemplation should be done while imagining oneself to be in the presence of the Creator or, at least, as a humble supplicant to the sacred mysteries. While approaching the realms of the spirit, right motive is of paramount importance.

The goal of our spiritual teachers is, like all teachers, for us to become self-reliant, in this case spiritually self-reliant. Thus, they do not wish to instruct us so much as enable us to instruct ourselves. This is why their communication takes place at a higher level, or usually does. By elevating our mind to the place they can be found, we become responsive to the quality of the higher worlds and start to build that quality into ourselves. By seeking their advice in the heart, we start to awaken the heart and become able to think in the heart which is the spiritual goal. Heart thinking is spiritual thinking and the way forward, as far as that is concerned, is through love. Love of God, love of Creation, love of the good, the beautiful and the true. If you don't have this love you must aspire to it. You must see its lack in yourself and pray to be given it. Only then can you really awaken spiritually and start to enter the world where your teachers await and seek to greet you as loving brothers and sisters.

Demons and Conspiracy Theories

It has often been observed that liberalism is both a symptom and a cause of a decaying civilisation and that neither it nor any ideological system inspired by it can actually build or preserve a civilisation worthy of the name. This has been the case in the past, and it is certainly the case now. But now there is something else. On previous occasions something like liberalism has arisen when a society has built itself up and reached a certain level of prosperity and comfort. It is, if you like, a self-indulgence that is basically parasitic on the work, creativity and energy of previous generations. A luxury that a wealthy and successful society can afford, or thinks it can. We have that today, but we also have something not so much in evidence at the time of the collapse of previous civilisations, though I am sure it was present. But it was not present to such a high degree.

I am talking about what I have talked about earlier in this book, and that is demonic corruption. I mention this again because I see it as the root cause of everything negative. Actually, the real root cause is human egotism and selfishness, as without that the corruption would have nothing to work on, no ground in which its seeds could sprout. Unto the pure all things are pure. However, if we are looking for the driving force behind the spiritual degradation of the 21st century, we must look beyond this world to the supernatural.

It is a fallacy to think there is material and there is spiritual, and the latter is always closer to truth. It may be less restricted in terms of the constituents of which is it formed but it is by no means necessarily morally better, any more than the mind is always good. The spiritual in this sense is a mental world and so can be as good or evil as the mind can be. It is useful to think of the spiritual world as extending vertically in a similar way to how the physical world extends horizontally, though with the difference that the various levels of being or consciousness, whatever you want to call it, are separated from one another by the quality of their spiritual vibration, their intrinsic openness to the full reality of God. We can with perfect justification talk about higher and lower in this context, and there is a moral value to these terms.

The lower levels are where the demons exist, the only place they can. They have cut themselves off from the light and life of God but continue to perpetuate themselves by stealing energy from human beings in incarnation. Ancient blood sacrifices come to mind as serving this need, and in the modern world I would surmise that the abortion of unborn infants does, too, but there is also 'negative energy' of any sort, anger, hatred and the like, which the demons can use and absorb to sustain themselves. Because they are so low themselves, they can only feed on energy that is of a similar low quality, but it is, at least, divine energy, even if misdirected and made unclean.

This may seem like science fiction but ask yourself this: What are demons? They are clearly fallen souls that have exiled themselves from God. But God is life. How then do they get life? They must steal it from those that have it, and they can only do this if they influence souls who still can draw life from God to 'lower their vibration'.

* * *

I have always fought shy of conspiracy theories and for several reasons. Many of them seem far-fetched and the product of eccentrics with bees in their bonnets who home in on isolated aspects of the world in which we live and ignore the overall picture. I have also been more influenced than I probably should have been by the pseudo-sophisticated attitude that smiles at people with tinfoil helmets and knows so much better because we're all rational now, aren't we? Mostly, though, it is because conspiracy theories are normally focused on the political and my interests have always been in the spiritual.

But there are multiple problems with this approach. For one thing, the Bible, especially the New Testament and specifically the Book of Revelation, is one long conspiracy theory. If you are a Christian, a real one, then you are a conspiracy theorist. No two ways about it. We live in a world of spiritual warfare in which demonic powers seek to corrupt God's creation, in particular that most important part of it which is the human race.

The second reason is of more recent development. The political has spilled over into the spiritual, using that word to describe the essential part of what makes human beings human. The dreadful lie that everything is political has taken root and is believed because the spiritual has been more or less chased off the face of the Earth, certainly insofar as it might have any meaning or real relevance to life. Everything is really spiritual, but everything has been made political now, even what used to be regarded as just social or cultural issues, even marriage, even the weather. This means that a spiritually concerned person has to take note of what is going on in the world today and cannot retreat to a position of inward detachment as might have been feasible at one time.

The third reason I have become drawn to the conspiracy theory point of view is the present time. In all seriousness, how can anyone not look at what has happened to the world since the beginning of 2020 (accompanied, coincidentally or not by a Saturn/Pluto conjunction throughout the year) and fail to see the deep manipulation of human beings that makes them participants in their own enslavement? Why do more people not see it? The only explanation I can come up with is that we have been so softened by relentless propaganda in all fields, from education to entertainment to politics to science and even many supposed spiritual teachings over the last 100 years that we are easy pickings unless we have some solid grounding in real religion and by that I mean, as far as the West is concerned, Christianity. Other contemporary spiritual approaches will not save us from sin and evil because they can all be accommodated into those things. Only the light of Christ is strong enough to resist them which, by the way, is a very good argument for the truth of Christ. But we don't believe that there is a conspiracy because our understanding of the nature of the world is so hopelessly compromised. There can't be a conspiracy because we live in a universe that is random and without meaning. Therefore, even when the fact of a conspiracy should be self-evident, we cannot accept it because it would call into question all our assumptions about the non-spiritual nature of life.

In the past I have, for reasons given above, inclined towards the popular view that things go wrong more because of human stupidity and greed than because of some dastardly plot. And if you are looking at the picture from a purely human perspective, that may well be so. But you cannot just look at things from that perspective. The real plot is supernatural. The relatively long time span during which all the pieces have been manoeuvred into place proves that even if nothing else does. Plenty else does though. There has been a relentless whittling away at spiritual truths and their replacement with anti-spiritual and, more recently, anti-natural values, if values is even the right word. For they are actually non-values whose only real purpose is to oppose real values. But they have become accepted because we have lost our moorings in transcendent reality so have no grounding in anything real. We can be pushed in any direction because nothing actually means anything. This is always the case when a society loses faith in God. And that means that such a society is destined to go. It will collapse either from external attack or internal decay or both. Ours is no exception to that rule.

Spiritually, things will not get better. They will continue

to deteriorate even if many of us will not recognise it as deterioration. We will all perceive the growing shadow in our minds and the constrictions in our lives, but those of us without faith will either not acknowledge their cause or else think this is how things have always been. Dissatisfaction, anger and hatred will spread but be regarded as righteous. Everything is somebody else's fault. The darkness in the world will grow. But this is actually a cause for optimism. Yes, it really is! There is nothing eternal in this world, and not meant to be, but when outward things are this bad it means, paradoxically, that God is not far away. He is causing us to turn away from the wreckage of this world and towards him, the only place where truth and goodness and real beauty abide everlastingly. As the world descends further into lies and spiritual oppression and most people accept that because it appears to offer them safety and security and they have no faith in anything higher, remember that important truth. When the world turns dark, we must hold fast to our inner knowledge of the light that shines just beyond its horizon. This is the most important lesson currently being taught in the earthly school.

The End of School

Many people seem to accept that we are living in extraordinary times. What is not generally understood is why that is. The collapse of the old order and traditional ways of understanding are recognised but there is the belief that things will get better as we move into a new era in which technology and political liberalism combine to free humanity from past superstitions and prejudices. So ignorant are we of metaphysical reality that we think the very things that damage us, perhaps even in some cases, if followed to excess, that damn us, are the cure for our malaise. Such is the extent of the deception practised on a foolish and unwary generation.

I say generation, but this has been a long time coming. In one sense, at least 2,000 years, but more especially we can date the descent, and overall descent it is despite a corresponding ascent in certain areas of life, from the end of the 18th century when some of the unexpected results of the Enlightenment, in itself a good thing, began to make their presence known. The French Revolution was a decisive break with the past. Ostensibly a movement for the liberation of the masses and curbing of priestly power (and no one is denying these things needed to happen), it was actually more about establishing the anti-principle of atheism and making this world the focus of our attention. It was the start of the sin of replacing the spiritual with the political. That has continued ever since and reached some kind of apotheosis, to use a completely inappropriate word, in our own time. Now the spiritual is given minimal importance and regarded, if regarded at all, as totally peripheral to the main issues of life. Where it exists, it has generally been absorbed into the concept of therapy, the relieving of pain and providing of pleasure for the earthly human being. Religions are shadows of their former selves, led in many cases by functionaries whose main purpose appears to be the continuation of the organisation, and whose understanding of life appears to differ in little appreciable sense from that of the secular powers.

What this means is that every individual is thrown back on himself. Every man and every woman has constantly to examine his or her own heart and conscience and cannot rely on outer guidance. Guidance is there, but it is not in the institutions of humanity, and even where it exists, it cannot be followed slavishly. It must always be interpreted in the light of personal understanding. That decidedly does not mean that we make our own reality, but we are responsible for ourselves and must forge our own inner understanding. How else can it be ours, and if it's not ours what is it worth? An additional complication is that most of the external forces now will point us in completely the wrong direction. They are not just neutral. They have been corrupted. But this may actually be helpful. Once we accept this is the case, we have no choice but to go within.

In a way this is what happens when we sit our final exams at the end of the education process. Help in the form of teachers, textbooks and the like is removed. It is just us, and that is the test of our real knowledge and ability to present it. We have a similar situation now. We must show that our spiritual orientation is true despite all the forces attempting to push it in the wrong direction. If we are made of the proper stuff and respond to the voice of God rather than that of the self or the world, we will come good and demonstrate that we are spiritually justified, worthy to enter the kingdom of God to which no one can gain entry whose heart is not already there.

I said that guidance still exists even if it is not to be found in human institutions or philosophies or even creeds. If someone asked me where they could find truth in this age of multiple competing philosophies, though many of them are really just variations on a similar theme, I would point them to the gospels and, most specifically, the gospel of St John. In this small work we have, I believe, the most authentic teaching and representation of Christ. But Christ was not primarily a teacher. He was, as John says, the Word of God made flesh. What does that mean?

God the Father has no body and cannot be bound by form in any way but he does have a human face and that is Christ, the Son who came to this world as a man and who united in his being the two poles of reality, spirit and matter. We all do this, but Christ did it in perfection thus paving the way for all who follow him to do the same in and through him. Thus, while the teaching he gave is important and should certainly be followed, the real lesson of Christ is in his person. If you can respond to Christ the Son of God as a real and living person the way is open for you to, I cannot put it any other way, absorb his vibration and start to be transformed. I believe this is the basis of the sacrament of Holy Communion which, not being a Catholic, I cannot take literally but which is clearly deeply symbolic. The essence of Christ is not his teaching but is his actual person. This is the almost magical reality of the Incarnation, that through accepting Christ we start to become like him. This takes us beyond other spiritual approaches because it involves stamping the living image of the incarnate God on our heart as opposed to approaching him through an earthly or even spiritual representation. That is good but it is not the same.

But be careful. I am not simply referring to believing in Jesus or if I am it is a spiritual belief I am talking about not an intellectual or emotionally based one. And that means it is responding to the true Christ who dwells in our heart not the, dare I say it, idol of Christ that human beings have made up from the stories in the Bible and the teachings of religion and religion itself. There is an earthly Christ, a Christ made by humans, and a divine one, and it is only the latter that can free us from death and sin and our own egos. He dwells in the highest heaven but he is also in the human heart, which is where we must look for him if we wish to truly know him. We can approach Christ through scripture, through religion, even through traditional art, but these are all external things. We can only really begin to know him as he is through an encounter that takes place deep within our own soul.

Everything in the material universe has a beginning, middle and end. As we saw in the Cycles of Changes chapter, we are currently nearing the culminating point of a long sequence of events. We think things have always been like this because we have no experience of other times except through the lens of history. To be sure, there have long been people who preached the end of the world, sometimes comically so. The idea has always been around because we have been in the Kali Yuga for a long time and the Kali Yuga as a whole is a kind of end times cycle. But now the process is accelerating, and the speed has really picked up since the turn of the millennium or perhaps since the solar eclipse and Grand Cross of August 1999 which I have long felt to be significant markers. The latter involved all the major planets except Pluto forming squares or oppositions to each other in one of the four fixed signs of the zodiac. Be that as it may, this was certainly a time when the world turned a corner and any spiritual legacy from the past finally disappeared.

More recent events have again moved the process along considerably. We have entered a period of soft totalitarianism (soft for the moment) and slipped to a new spiritual low which everyone should register on some level, but most will not be able to recognise. How can those without spiritual understanding find the intellectual tools to perceive what is taking place? They have no point of reference. This is the tragedy of our time. We are caught in a spiritual trap which we do not see because we lack the metaphysical framework that would enable us to identify it for what it is.

Except that we don't. Certainly, we may not have an outer belief structure, though these obviously exist and in plain sight.

But we do have the truth within us and that is the test of this gathering in period. Are we able to reject the lies of the world and turn to this inner knowledge or are we so attached to our worldly pleasures, attachments, prejudices and desires that we reject anything higher? It cannot be stressed too much that this is a time of testing and the results of these tests will have a real bearing on our future. Our inner worth is being examined. It is not how moral we are that matters. It is not what we may know or not know. It is not even if we are spiritual. That may just reflect our desires and ambitions. It is whether we love God. That love may not always take an obvious form but God will know what is in the heart, which is the only place he looks. If you love him, you will be with him. Now is the concluding point of a long span of years. This is a time that really matters. If that makes you stop and consider where you stand, good. If you currently reject it as superstitious fantasy, don't reject it out of hand. It may be that as events unfold it will begin to make more sense.

Appendix - Meeting the Masters Talk

This is the edited text of a talk I gave at a conference in 2019 on my book *Meeting the Masters*. It will be familiar stuff for those who have read that book but those who haven't might be interested to learn something about the original inspiration behind the present work.

* * *

My subject today is spiritual teachers and when I say spiritual, I mean those who speak from the spiritual world and who can be thought of by virtue of that as messengers from God, bearing witness to his existence. I know this field is full of all sorts of weird and wonderful things, a lot more weird than wonderful if we're honest, but let me tell you something of my own experience, which I'd like to share because I think that if we knew there were genuine spiritual beings who watched over us and guided us as far as they were able to within the confines of spiritual law and free will, that would be a great encouragement to us in our labours in this world.

My story goes back 40 years. At the time I was a young man dissatisfied with conventional life. I had a job that bored me, prospects of a sort that didn't interest me and I was searching for something more than a mundane existence dedicated to material success, which was pretty much all that was on offer then as far as I knew. I had a limited knowledge of the spiritual movements that were beginning to coalesce into what became known as the New Age but found them fairly shallow, full of extravagant claims that were not borne out either by the followers or the leaders. Religion, such as I knew it, seemed moribund and concerned with something far off. I wasn't particularly interested in what happened after death. I wanted life to have some real meaning and purpose now.

One day, in my lunch hour, I wandered into a metaphysical bookshop near where I worked in London and began to browse, looking for something that might provide answers to questions I hadn't even properly framed yet. As I searched through the shelves a man beside me spoke, asking whether he might make a recommendation or two. He'd seen I didn't really know what I was looking for and wondered if I'd like some help. Overcoming my natural reticence in such circumstances, I agreed. He was friendly and we got talking and I was sufficiently interested to accept his offer of lunch, during which we discussed such subjects as meditation, vegetarianism and reincarnation, none of which were quite as mainstream then as they are now.

It turned out that this man, Michael Lord by name, had led quite an interesting life. He was then 58 years old and had packed a lot into his time. Born in 1919, he spent his childhood in England, France and Switzerland before being sent to India at the outbreak of the Second World War where, amongst other things, he was ADC to Lord Wavell who was the Viceroy before Mountbatten. When the war was over, he went to America where he ran some kind of fashionable country club near New York. But after a few years he got fed up with high society life and returned to England. Going from one extreme to the other, he converted to Catholicism and became a Benedictine monk at Ealing Abbey. But this didn't work out because in that particular order he would have had to have become a priest, which he didn't want to do, so he left. The other problem was that he was interested in Eastern religion, which didn't really sit well in that time and place. He had nothing but praise for his fellow monks but knew that life was not for him.

Going back into the world, he became the secretary of a political club in London during the '60s, though a less political person I can't imagine, where he again mixed with the establishment elite of the day. He then went to India and was initiated by a swami in the Ramakrishna order. He stayed there for several months then returned to England. He lived in Cornwall for a bit as an antiques dealer, ran a shop selling crystals just before the fashion for them took off and then went back to India. He used to say that though he was born in England, he had been conceived in India and that had left its mark on him. When I met him he had just come back from Bombay, as it was known then, where he had run a guest house for the Hare Krishnas (as a non-member) but left because he got fed up with the infighting and jockeying for position. The last straw apparently was a knife fight outside the temple.

I've given you a brief resumé of Michael's background in view of what comes later on in this story. He was a typical what used to be called seeker after truth and had looked in many places but never found what he was looking for. Unlike most people who either give up or make do and stay where they are, he had always moved on. You might think that shows a certain restlessness or even superficiality on his part but some people have an inner drive that won't let them be satisfied with what doesn't feel right, and I think that was his case.

So that's Michael. After our initial encounter in the bookshop I met up with him a few more times for further discussions and the eventual outcome of all that was that several months later the two of us were living in Bath, running an antiques shop by day and meditating in the evening. I had given up my job and decided to throw in my lot with him, the two of us leading a life dedicated to the spiritual quest though, it has to be said, without much outer structure. He was now 59 and I was 23, so as you can imagine my family and friends were not enthusiastic. In fact, "Are you mad?" was one of the more restrained responses. Michael's family consisted of one cousin who was a retired army colonel and who reacted as you might think a retired army colonel might react, but we became friends later on when we got to know each other. In spite of all this opposition, sometimes you have to do what you feel is right and, for me, this was one of those times. Michael, I think, was also quite taken aback by how things had turned out but he had lived much of his life by instinct and followed the path as it appeared before him so he was more used to unconventional ways.

For a few weeks we led this life uneventfully. I enjoyed living in Bath, which is certainly one of the places where the sense of Albion, the sacred counterpart to Britain, can break through, and the antiques world had rather more colourful characters in it than the Civil Service where I had previously worked. I was reading spiritual books and learning about the various approaches to the search for God and I was practising meditation with the vague idea that one day I might break through into some kind of higher consciousness, though I remember Michael tactfully warning me that things weren't quite that simple. But I had the enthusiasm and naivety of the neophyte. And then something rather unusual happened.

We were sitting in meditation as we did every evening at around 9 o'clock, when Michael suddenly began to chant what sounded like the OM, the Hindu sacred sound that is supposed to symbolise ultimate truth. It's very similar to the ison or drone in Byzantine chant. He had never done this before, and it resonated throughout the room in our small flat. The sound went on and on and when it eventually ceased the room had a totally different atmosphere, as though it had been ritually cleansed and purified. There was a presence to it and the silence that ensued seemed a real thing rather than a simple absence of noise. Then Michael began to speak. Except it wasn't him speaking.

The words were coming from his mouth, but they were not in his voice. They were spoken without hesitation and with an authority that should have quelled doubt. But, of course, I did doubt. I was, and remain, a fairly sceptical person. That was what put me off the New Age type teachers I mentioned earlier. At first, I thought Michael might be putting on a show but the words, the sense of presence, never mind subsequent experiences and my knowledge of his character, showed this to be impossible. It wasn't Michael. Then I thought that maybe the voice could be that of a real spirit but of the kind contacted in spiritualism, that's to say, not a very elevated being. I had once been to a seance at the Spiritualist Association in London so had encountered this sort of thing before. But that wasn't possible either. The whole tone of the communication, the power, the deep sense of wisdom and love, all showed this to be a spirit of real substance, an exemplar of deep truth. You'll have to take my word for this, but I am not someone who is easily impressed. I was more than impressed by this. I was humbled.

I don't much remember much of what was said on that first occasion. Thereafter I kept notes scribbled down after the talk had ended, while it was still fresh in my mind, but I didn't think it would be very respectful to dash out of the room for pen and paper while it was still going on. However, I do recall that it was mostly an introductory talk. I was greeted not by my name but simply as 'my child'. Interestingly, in all the years they spoke to me they never used my name, and nor did they ever use Michael's name when they referred to him, generally calling him 'our brother'. The essence of what he said was that he was pleased Michael and I had made the decision to live together. We had been sent to each other and we would be guided in our spiritual endeavours. I got the impression this was something that had been set up long ago.

From then on, this being and others like him spoke to me through Michael on a regular basis. They would come during our period of meditation and speak for between 10 and 20 minutes. Their subject was mostly the lessons I was here to learn, and they were compassionate but exacting teachers. When I asked them who or what they were they told me to think of them as messengers from God but never gave a name, though I did ask.

Actually, on one occasion I was told a name, of which more later. But I think the general no name policy was because names would bring the experience down to a more mundane level and so detract from the spiritual message. Look at some of the fancy names and grandiose titles supposedly higher beings do give themselves in the channelling literature. But names aside, from certain things they said, I understood they were souls who lived beyond this mortal world, existing in higher spheres which they described in terms of light, beauty, colour and spiritual glory. They were what is known as Masters.

Now, unfortunately this word, Masters, has a certain amount of baggage attached to it, as indeed do spiritualist or channelling type communications. Regarding the word, they used it of themselves and as I stood to them in the role of a pupil, it's appropriate. But it calls to mind the Theosophists and groups deriving from that line of occult thought, and the beings who spoke to me don't seem to have much in common with those worthies. They didn't give me any elaborate esoteric teachings, as people are often disappointed to find, or talk about a New Age or higher consciousness or anything of that sort of thing. No big revelations or world-transforming philosophies. Nothing dramatic. Most of the time they restricted themselves to specific spiritual instruction, tailored to my needs.

As for the connection with channelling and spiritualism, this is something I have always fought shy of. You might wonder why, given there clearly is a connection in terms of the mechanism of the operation, but it comes down to the quality of the communication. In my experience the great majority of channelled messages have very limited value and can even be serious distractions, if not lures, into spiritual blind alleys. Even when you might accept there is something genuine going on, not influenced by the medium's own mind, the communicating entities do not seem of a very high spiritual standard. They may exist in a world beyond this one but that does not mean they have a real proximity to God.

It is often stated by esotericists that high spiritual beings do not communicate through mediums, that being an atavistic practice restricted to spirits still functioning in the lower levels of non-physical reality. And I agree with this statement. The goal of teachers of this sort is to educate their pupils spiritually, not intellectually, and so they teach through impressing ideas on the pupil's higher mind, which it is then the pupil's responsibility to pick up on and interpret according to his capacity. In point of fact, my instructors told me that this was their aim. But there are exceptions to the general rule, and I am bound to say I believe this to be one of them. Of course, such an assertion can't be proved but I do think that anyone who reads their words should be able to sense something of their quality.

I should mention something of the nature of Michael's mediumship. He was quite unconscious during the process. He told me he would be lifted out of his body and then feel surrounded by an atmosphere of love before returning, which was always painful for him, a jarring re-entry to lower vibrations to use that terminology. Sometimes, he would have fallen over if I hadn't been prepared to catch him, as I was told by the Masters to be ready to do. He'd ask for a drink of water and it took him several minutes to come to. When he was gone, his body would sit bolt upright like one of those ancient Egyptian statues. His eyes would be closed, and he remained completely still except for the moving of his lips. The voice that spoke was not his at all, not the timbre, not the accent, nothing. Michael had a middle-class, English accent but the accent of the Masters speaking through him was not an English one. But then it was not an identifiably foreign one either. It was of someone who spoke perfect English in an idiomatic English style but who you could tell wasn't a native Englishman. They didn't all speak in the same way, I could generally tell the difference, but there was a similarity of tone. In the book I wrote about them I said that their vocal delivery was strong, measured and assured, almost solemn on occasion, but never in the slightest bit stiff or pompous. They never rushed and they never hesitated.

I have heard recordings of mediumistic seances in which a spirit is supposedly talking. Often it seems to be in quite a mechanical tone of voice or ponderous and stilted, not really human sometimes. This was nothing like that. It was perfectly natural without any portentousness to it. It wasn't normal but it was natural.

Michael was not aware of what was spoken through him and if I asked did he want to know, he expressed no interest. It was for me, he said. I asked him how long he had known of the existence of the Masters, and if and how they spoke to him. He said they had contacted him first around the time of our meeting but not fully made themselves known to him until we started living together. They spoke to him clairaudiently or sometimes he would just hear a voice 'inside his head'. On occasion, he also saw beautiful faces. Michael was not an intellectual type of person by any means and he didn't analyse what he experienced but he had good spiritual instincts and, most of all, a great capacity for love. It was that, so the Masters told me, that enabled them to use him as their medium.

I don't know if any of you are familiar with a couple of books written by Swami Omananda, actually an Irishwoman called Maud McCarthy. They describe how a protegé of hers, known simply as the Boy, was used as a medium by the Masters, though much more extensively and publicly than Michael was, during the 1930s and '40s. His character, its simplicity, straight-forwardness and integrity, coupled with a spiritual temperament quite uninterested in abstract speculation and theory, reminds me very much of how Michael was. The Boy was from a working class background, whereas Michael was upper middle class and had led quite a sophisticated life, mixing on familiar terms with many of the well-known people of his day, but there always remained a kind of innocence about him which endeared him to some people but made others think he was a bit of a fool. I prefer to say he retained a child-like quality all his life and I think that's what made him useable by the Masters. Our analytical brain is a great gift if we want to get things done in the physical world but it can block out the pure simplicity of spiritual truth if it gets out of hand, as it certainly has done in our day.

People ask me how do I know Michael wasn't just faking the whole thing. It's a fair question but it does presuppose a particularly devious personality and I know that just wasn't him. Besides, if he could have faked the depth of wisdom and spiritual authority that came through him, he could have cleaned up on the guru trail. I'm not joking. I've seen a fair number of gurus and holy men in this world and none of them could hold a candle to the Masters. Moreover, this carried on from 1979 to 1999, though it was much reduced after the early years. There would have been no reason for him to keep doing it other than some kind of deep-rooted psychological problem which it was obvious he didn't have. I didn't live with Michael because supernatural voices told me to. They did say that was their desire for our mutual benefit, but they left me free to do as I wished. They also pointed to flaws in his character that I might be able to help him with, though the chief aim of that was to teach me how to talk to others without criticising them, which they regarded as one of my faults.

If he wasn't faking, could it have been some kind of multiple personality thing or dissociative identity disorder? Well, it was multiple personality in that there were several beings who spoke through Michael but they were totally independent not split off aspects of his own self. I can say this with confidence because of the profound qualitative differences there were between them and him. They were far beyond him by every measure. Michael had no history of mental illness nor had there been any childhood trauma or abuse. He said he'd had a happy childhood and he gave no sign of being bipolar or depressive or schizophrenic or anything like that. He could be emotional at times but the Masters actually mentioned that this aspect of his character was linked to his mediumship.

I am firmly of the opinion that any unusual experience should be subjected to rigorous scrutiny but on this occasion it does seem as though the explanation offered by the voices themselves, the most straight-forward one really, is the true one.

At this point I should read out some of the things that were said to me by the Masters. As I said earlier, their intention was to instruct me spiritually. They didn't say much about themselves and they didn't give me any theoretical stuff, metaphysics about God or the universe or whatever. They left that for me to sort out for myself, though it was assumed that God was real and that the spiritual world was the true ground of this one. But their purpose was practical spiritual training, not to satisfy my curiosity about this or that. I kept notes of most of their talks during the first year, when they were at their most frequent. I did this less later on and I have lost the notebooks I used after the first one, but the general themes were similar so that's not as unfortunate as it might be.

Here's my log of one of the early talks. I had moved in with Michael on January 1st 1979, and this talk is dated 15th February so the talks might have been going on for a week or two at this stage. I was still being broken in, as one might put it.

The Master said he was pleased with my progress. He stressed the need to remain diligent and conscientious, and told me to keep on striving and forging ahead. My next trial would be in my relationship with Michael. Due to various experiences in his life, and the sort of life he has led, he has had to present a front to the world. This is necessary as, in his evolved state, lower vibrations could harm him. As I have not led a

sophisticated life, I might find this acting a role difficult to understand but it is with my assistance that Michael can find his true self. It is the will of the Masters that Michael and I help each other. I can help him find his true self through respect, understanding and love, while he can train me in the outer spiritual path. The Master said it was not necessary to inform Michael of the contents of this talk as they communicated with him separately.

I wrote down the Masters' words after the talk, so although I tried to keep their exact words as much as possible it's inevitable that some of this is expressed in my language. On the other hand, I did want to preserve the form of their delivery as best I could, as well as the substance and I would say most of this is as they spoke, albeit trimmed down to the essential.

What is being said here is twofold. There is encouragement and the attempt to stiffen my resolve for the life ahead, which is not going to be as rosy as I might have imagined. Like many people, I had thought that leading a spiritual life would be a matter of a speedy progression to the sunny uplands of joy and bliss etc. Ah, the naivety of the innocent! It's actually much more about a dredging up of all the darkness in one's soul and the confrontation with the reality of who you are. This is going to entail suffering and that's just how it is.

The second thing relates to me and Michael and our life together. We had joined forces, but we were two very different people. Different generations but also different types. Sometimes his behaviour annoyed me. It could seem worldly and at odds with our spiritual intentions. The Masters explained why that might be, but I was being told to develop tolerance.

Here's another talk from around the same time.

The Master warned me that from now on I must guard against

great joys as well as great depressions and should keep an even keel at all times. He said I should also guard against negative entities which will attack when I least expect it, in ways that I least expect. He told me to listen to Michael and remain with him for the present. It is they, the Masters, who have arranged this life together and though I may not understand it all now, things will become clearer later on. Michael is as he is because the Masters have arranged it for the purposes of teaching me. All is proceeding well and is guided and arranged by God and His Masters, who look forward to being reunited with me. He said it is not wrong for me to talk to Michael about aspects of his personality I think could be improved on but do it for his sake and the love of God, not because I want to change him or am irritated by him.

Here again there is encouragement and warning. What these write ups don't include are the questions I asked the Masters, though I incorporate their response. As I hinted, I sometimes found it difficult to get on with Michael in our daily life because of our different characters. I had probably asked for some advice on this score. But the Masters never pandered to my weaknesses. I was told that anything I said or did had to be for the right reason or else it just wouldn't work.

There is also a mention of negative entities and that these might attack. The Masters fully accepted the reality of evil, including supernatural evil, in our universe. They mentioned this on several occasions and warned that the more progress one made on the spiritual path, the more one would be attacked by evil. The form of attack might vary but was usually psychological, as in fanning the flames of negative characteristics such as anger, irritation, depression, hatred, etc until you get to the point where you identify with the emotion and start to become it. I was told to be aware of this and watch out for it within my mind. Evil can only work with what's there. If you expunge evil from your own heart, it is helpless, but evil is very subtle and as the Master said, will attack in ways you least expect at times when your defences might be down. I should add that once, after a talk, something really nasty got into Michael and physically attacked me. This apparently was a possibility due to his mediumistic tendency and the fact that after the Master left an evil spirit could, as it were, nip in before Michael got back. The Masters had helpers who functioned on lower planes than they themselves did and who were responsible for the smooth running of the operation but sometimes things could go wrong, though I only remember this happening once or twice. On this occasion it was soon dealt with by the helpers and the spirit expelled. This might sound rather outlandish but it's just how things are. In our day, few people are physically possessed by demons due to the lower levels of psychic polarisation. We are more mentally focused. On the other hand, I would say demons can influence us on both the intellectual and emotional levels and this is not uncommon. C.S. Lewis's book *The Screwtape Letters* might be fiction but it's not fantasy.

The Master says that he looks forward to being reunited with me. What this points to is the pre-existence of the soul. As far as I know, this is not accepted by Christianity, but it makes sense. Do we really think we began only in this life? Personally, I never have thought that and always regarded myself as having come here from somewhere else. I am not talking about reincarnation necessarily, but the truth is we are spiritual beings in earthly form, and we need to start coming to terms with the implications and responsibilities of that.

Here's the next talk.

The Master said I must have more control over my moodiness which was due to the fact I was in a young body. Rather than being swayed by moods I should ignore them. He said that

this would be the last talk for a while as Michael was getting too weak to be used as a medium for a while. The Masters would guide and protect us as long as we did their will, which was to live together in love and harmony. He would watch over our progress and come back at a later date. He said at this stage I should regard the Masters not as individuals but as messengers from God. He sent his love and blessings and the love of the higher Masters.

The Masters made clear that mediumship of this sort took a lot out of Michael and that I should never start taking it for granted. In this talk they also mention what they call the higher Masters confirming that there is hierarchy even in heaven, which is the traditional understanding as well. In fact, these higher Masters did talk to me as well occasionally, not often but now and then, and here is a record of a talk given by one of them.

I was talked to by one of the higher Masters. The feeling of power and majesty was almost overwhelming, but he spoke kindly and, unusually, even gave his name though it was not one I was familiar with. He told me that the body is a frame and its functions are not to be feared. He said it was designed for beings of a lesser evolution than myself and was more suited to their needs. He said that sometimes it is the will and not the action that counts and stressed I should avoid lassitude as I have important work to do. He told me to have faith, courage and determination and said that I was always protected by his helpers.

I need to say first of all, that the important work referred to just means the lessons I was learning at the time with Michael. Then I should say a word or two about the phrase 'lesser evolution'. It is a tenet of many spiritual philosophies that we come to Earth to develop our spiritual potential. So, this is not like random Darwinian evolution but more the gradual unfolding of qualities already present in embryo. As the Masters told me at other times, Earth is a school and we are here to learn. There are souls at different stages of learning, just as a school has different classes. Systems like the Indian caste system were originally based on that idea and though we have rejected these in favour of egalitarian democracy nowadays we need to understand that these were not just systems based on power and oppression, even if they could descend into that in a decadent phase, but said something important about how human beings are. A great and widely unrecognised flaw of the egalitarianism model is that when a society is hierarchically structured people look up, and this includes not just within the actual society itself but in terms of how it approaches art, religion and everything. In an egalitarian society, however, there is an inevitable tendency to the lowest common denominator and everything, art and religion included, is pulled down and vulgarised. Is this not painfully obvious in our modern world where the higher is debased and the lower praised?

When I wrote the book about my experience with the Masters I didn't mention the name I was given here but recently I was reading Tolkien's translation of the old English poem Beowulf and there is a section in the poem where Beowulf is compared to an ancient hero who was also a dragon slayer. That hero's name was Sigemund and this was the name given by the higher Master. At the time I wasn't familiar with the name and it meant nothing to me. I wrote it down phonetically as ' Siggermund'.

What I find intriguing in Tolkien's notes on the reference to Sigemund in his Beowulf translation is that he says this "is the oldest reference to the Sigemund story that is now extant, even in point of manuscript date." He makes this point because in later versions it is Sigemund's son, Siegfried, who kills the dragon, as also in Wagner. But Tolkien thinks these later accounts have embellished the story, as often happened with myths and legends which grew as they moved through time, and that Sigemund acquired a son who took over his exploits. So, for Tolkien, Sigemund not Siegfried is the original dragon slayer.

This is interesting to me because it gives the name extra significance. Sigemund is a kind of original hero of Northern European civilisation and the fact that this is the only name any of the Masters gave seems to have some relevance, to me at any rate. What is more, it was the name of one who was described as a higher Master and whose tone and manner were certainly that of a being of extraordinary power and authority. He didn't speak to me much, but I can still remember that it was like being in the presence of a great king.

Here's an excerpt from another talk.

I was told that it was very important that I always remembered the Creator, keeping Him in my thoughts at all times. Throughout the day I should constantly visualise a white light surrounding and protecting me. This is a very crucial period for me, and I was vulnerable to attacks from outward evil that would affect my thoughts if I let it. If antagonistic thoughts did arise, I should dispel them by concentrating on the Masters. I had to do my work in the market but should remain unattached to it. What we needed would be provided.

This speaks for itself for the most part. I would just draw attention to a couple of things. One is, remember the Creator. This is the simplest instruction but actually covers almost everything you need if you really do it. By fixing your mind on God you start to draw close to him and that very thought acts as a kind of purifying agent.

The second point is the remark that what we needed would be provided. We worked in an antiques market and had to make a profit through buying and selling antiques. That was the only source of our income, so we had to take it seriously. At the same time, it was only a means of making a living. The real work lay elsewhere. The fact is, what we needed was provided and I take this to mean that if you do dedicate yourself to God he'll look after you, though you should never just sit back and assume things will drop into your lap. Have confidence in God but don't ever take him for granted.

Next talk.

I was told that my life must continue in a routine, in fact, until I left my physical body. The Master said that they always knew what was in my mind, but it was up to me to broach a subject if I wanted to discuss it. They impressed things on me, but it was my responsibility to act on them. When I speak to Michael about things that I thought important, I should at all times do so calmly, so he would know that what I was saying came from deep intuition and not petty caprice. No-one can accept something that he is told angrily even if in his heart he knows that it is true.

As a point of interest, petty caprice is not a phrase Michael would ever have used. That's the case with a lot of words and phrases the Masters used.

I think I am running out of time, so I won't comment any further on the talks but here are excerpts from a few more. I haven't selected these for any particular reason. They are fairly typical.

The Master's message was that I should occupy myself during the day and not think so much. He said I dream and moon about too much and live too much in the mental. I must be more practical and learn to live on the earth plane. Again, he

said that I should work using my hands. Simple tasks were enough, but I should use them regularly. This was the best way for me to conquer my lack of humility. The Masters would think for me and I should follow them and not bother myself with a lot of theory. He was pleased by what he called my great love for Michael, as he said that we would be together for quite a while on Earth. My black moods are caused by the evil forces attacking me so I must keep myself busy, allowing myself no time to brood.

Michael and I were together for 21 years which is quite a while.

The Master said that at night we should attune ourselves to the higher planes by meditation or prayer so that when we left our bodies we could go there quickly and easily. He said that music was a wonderful medium, but I should not listen to it to excess as it tended to make me listless and dreamy. Earth is a school and I have work to do here. The wish to experience the glories of the higher planes was understandable but should not be indulged or the reason for being on Earth would be neglected. Now I needed to be earthed and that was one thing that Michael was there to help me with. He told me to be more simple and childlike adding, "Do not be as those who seek to penetrate to every corner of the universe but do not know themselves. It is not necessary to chase after the many mysteries of existence. Live simply in the heart and all mysteries will in time become known to you."

Many spiritually inclined people seek to escape the hard fact of this world, but we are here for a reason, to learn and to serve God wherever he may put us. Joy may come but we should not have it as a priority or reason to seek God.

I asked if constantly thinking of beauty was an unwise habit and he replied that this was natural in a spiritual person but that I should project beauty and not dwell on it. He told me that beauty is everywhere. It varies in degrees according to its closeness to God but there is God in everything and that means beauty. Do not love one thing and despise everything else because it does not match up to what you love. Accept everything on its merits, not judging it or comparing it with more evolved things or the higher planes. Be detached from your surroundings and feel the humility of accepting gratefully whatever God offers you.

Well, there we are. These are a few excerpts from some of the talks that took place during the first year of the process. The fact of the reality of these beings I have called Masters tells us something about the universe. It is a spiritual universe. The physical world in which we live is merely the lowest level of a multi-dimensional reality with the higher worlds being worlds of greater light, freedom, beauty and consciousness. We can attain these higher worlds through proper spiritual development, and we have help in this, let's be frank, difficult task. We may not be aware of this help in our conscious minds but if we seek to attune ourselves correctly through humility, meditation and prayer, then we can render ourselves susceptible to divine influence, which will prompt us along the right path. But this is not a passive thing. We are only ever guided. Our will is our own. The most important thing we can do is to make the right choices.

The book I wrote about this I called *Meeting the Masters*. It mostly describes the first year of the experience, when the communications were at their most frequent. They actually lasted for 21 years and stopped just before the end of the last millennium when Michael died. Since then I have had no outer contact with the Masters, nor sought any, but I try to put into practice what they taught me and that is a constantly ongoing process. I have been fortunate enough to have had living proof of the reality of the spiritual world and would like to pass that on to anyone else who might be interested.

* * *

This was the point at which the talk ended. During the question and answer session that followed I was asked what relation there might be, if any, between the Masters who spoke to me and Christ. I replied that Jesus was the one religious personage the Masters ever spoke of by name and added my conviction that though they never mentioned this, they were his disciples. But the matter was not discussed, and it is not their way to force beliefs of any kind on their pupils as their goal is to make the student spiritually self-aware.

However, I mentioned earlier the parallel experience of Maud McCarthy and the Boy. At the end of her book *Towards the Mysteries* there is a very moving passage in which she questions her Master on precisely this subject. She asks whether it was from Christ and as his messengers that the Masters came. The Master (and I quote) *"paused in thought; pondered long, and seemed to hesitate. Presently he nodded slowly, and breathed: **Yes, he sent us out.**"* This echoes my belief.

About the author

William Wildblood was born in London. After a period working as an antiques dealer, he left the UK to run a guesthouse in South India. He later moved to France where he was an occasional guide at the medieval abbey of le Mont Saint-Michel. He returned to England at the end of the 20th century, working for various magazines including seven years as an antiques columnist. He has written several other books including *Meeting the Masters* and *Remember the Creator*.

EXPLORING THE WORLD OF HIDDEN KNOWLEDGE

Axis Mundi Books provide the most revealing and coherent explorations and investigations of the world of hidden or forbidden knowledge. Take a fascinating journey into the realm of Esoteric Mysteries, High Magic (non-pagan), Mysticism, Mystical Worlds, Goddess, Angels, Aliens, Archetypes, Cosmology, Alchemy, Gnosticism, Theosophy, Kabbalah, Secret Societies and Religions, Symbolism, Quantum Theory, Conspiracy Theories, Apocalyptic Mythology, Unexplained Phenomena, Holy Grail and Alternative Views of Mainstream Religion.

If you have enjoyed this book, why not tell other readers by posting a review on your preferred book site? Recent bestsellers from Axis Mundi Books are:

On Dragonfly Wings
A Skeptic's Journey to Mediumship
Daniela I. Norris

Daniela Norris, former diplomat and atheist, discovers communication with the other side following the sudden death of her younger brother.
Paperback: 978-1-78279-512-4 ebook: 978-1-78279-511-7

Inner Light

The Self-Realization via the Western Esoteric Tradition
P.T. Mistlberger
A comprehensive course in spiritual development using the
powerful teachings of the Western esoteric tradition.
Paperback: 978-1-84694-610-3 ebook: 978-1-78279-625-1

The Seeker's Guide to Harry Potter

Dr Geo Trevarthen
An in-depth analysis of the mythological symbols and themes
encountered in the Harry Potter series, revealing layers of meaning
beneath the surface of J K Rowling's stories.
Paperback: 978-1-84694-093-4 ebook: 978-1-84694-649-3

The 7 Mysteries

Your Journey from Matter to Spirit
Grahame Martin
By simply reading this book you embark on a journey of
transformation from the world of matter into spirit.
Paperback: 978-1-84694-364-5

Angel Healing & Alchemy

How To Begin Melchisadec, Sacred Seven & the Violet Ray
Angela McGerr
Angelic Healing for physical and spiritual harmony.
Paperback: 978-1-78279-742-5 ebook: 978-1-78279-337-3

Colin Wilson's 'Occult Trilogy'

A Guide for Students
Colin Stanley
An essential guide to Colin Wilson's major writings on the occult.
Paperback: 978-1-84694-706-3 ebook: 978-1-84694-679-0

The Heart of the Hereafter
Love Stories from the End of Life
Marcia Brennan
This book can change not only how we view the end of life, but
how we view life itself and the many types of love we experience.
Paperback: 978-1-78279-528-5 ebook: 978-1-78279-527-8

Kabbalah Made Easy
Maggy Whitehouse
A down to earth, no-red-strings-attached look at the mystical
tradition made famous by the Kabbalah Center.
Paperback: 978-1-84694-544-1 ebook: 978-1-84694-890-9

The Whole Elephant Revealed
Insights Into the Existence and Operation of Universal Laws and
the Golden Ratio
Marja de Vries
An exploration of the universal laws which make up the dynamic
harmony and balance of the universe.
Paperback: 978-1-78099-042-2 ebook: 978-1-78099-043-9

Readers of ebooks can buy or view any of these bestsellers by
clicking on the live link in the title. Most titles are published in
paperback and as an ebook. Paperbacks are available in traditional
bookshops. Both print and ebook formats are available online.
Find more titles and sign up to our readers' newsletter at
http://www.johnhuntpublishing.com/mind-body-spirit
Follow us on Facebook at https://www.facebook.com/OBooks and
Twitter at https://twitter.com/obooks